The Bicycle Commuting Book

S0-BIL-234

5/2

# The
# Bicycle Commuting Book

## Using the bicycle for utility and transportation

Right-hand traffic edition

## Rob Van der Plas

Illustrated by the author

Bicycle Books — San Francisco

copyright © Robert van der Plas, 1989

Printed in the USA

Published by:
Bicycle Books, Inc. P.O. Box 2038
Mill Valley, CA 94941

Distributed to the book trade by:
(USA)      The Talman Company, New York, NY
(Canada)  Raincoast Book Distributing, Vancouver, BC
(UK)       Chris Lloyd Sales and Marketing Services, Poole, Dorset *


Cover photograph:
Rob van der Plas


Frontispiece photograph:
Ben Swets

**Library of Congress Cataloging in Publication Data**
Van der Plas, Robert, 1938—
The Bicycle Commuting Book, Using the bicycle for utility and transportation
Bibliography: p. Includes index
1. Bicycles and bicycling — manuals, handbooks, etc.
2. Bicycle commuting — manuals, handbooks, etc.
3. Authorship — manuals, handbooks, etc.
I. Title

Library of Congress Catalog Card Number 89-61364

ISBN 0-933201-19-2 Paperback original

* The British (LH-traffic) edition of this book is available as ISBN 0-933201-29-X

# About the Author

Rob Van der Plas is a professional engineer and a lifelong commuting cyclist who has written about the subject for specialized magazines since 1975. His many books about various aspects of bicycling have appeared in the US, Great Britain, Germany and Holland, while some were translated into French, Spanish, Danish and Swedish.

In his native Holland, he used the bicycle to get around for work and pleasure, a habit he kept up when he moved to Great Britain in 1960 and even when he settled in the US in 1968.

Working for a major oil company, he was at the time seen as a kind of subversive on account of his curious mode of transportation. But that changed drastically at the time of the first oil crunch, when it suddenly became patriotic to conserve the same resources that had been squandered so thoughtlessly before. Now it was possible to get bicycle storage facilities, showers and dressing rooms for those who chose to ride their bikes to work.

Though as keen as anybody to lead an environmentally responsible life, the real reasons he still cycles to work should not be lost: it's enjoyable, practical and convenient.

# Preface

This book wants to sell you on an old idea: the bicycle as a practical means of transportation. Once forgotten altogether, at least in the US and most other English-speaking countries, the bicycle has found a renewed acceptance in recent years. But it has largely been restricted to its use as a recreational vehicle.

Yet the bicycle's *alter ego* — as a practical vehicle — is at least as important. In view of the ever increasing automotive congestion and the threat motorized transportation forms to our environment, the bicycle's practical advantages may become more and more apparent in the future. Advantages not just to society at large, but also to the individual user.

However, this book is not merely an argument for increased bicycle use: it is above all a practical guide that shows how to go about it. After all, some of us have been doing it for many years, while most other cyclists — even if they may merrily ride a hundred miles or more at the weekend — feel inhibited about riding to work. And then there are those who do not really feel fully at ease on the bike at all. Both groups will learn many useful skills and get helpful insights from this book.

As always, some readers may have comments about subjects not covered adequately. You may have suggestions for improving the book or illustrations that would clarify some of the issues covered. You are invited to address any contributions of this kind to the author, c/o Bicycle Books (see copyright page for address).

# Table of Contents

# 1. Why Bike to Work?

Let me ask you another question: why not? Why drive a car to work, why go on the bus, ride the underground? Bicycling is a fast and convenient way of getting around, though that seems to be overlooked at a time when riding a bike is supposed to be *fun*. Unless you're exceptionally fortunate, driving a car to work, a bus, the underground won't be fun. Riding a bike can be. It certainly is invigorating, healthy. No other way of getting to work comes close.

Millions of Americans have bought fancy bikes in recent years. They've added equally fancy gadgets and wear fancy bicycle clobber. Because it's fun, because it's healthy, because it's *in* to ride a bike. Yet many of them rarely really use their bikes. Their fashionable outfits go out of style long before they are worn out. Not enough time to ride.

The hours that they are short are spent doing serious things, things that are neither fun nor healthy. Like driving their car to work, or waiting for the bus. The average American adult spends 1.5 hours a day cummuting and another hour driving here or there for other supposedly practical purposes. That's two and one half hours of lost freedom. One hundred and fifty minutes a day; nearly a thousand hours a year. And of those many wasted hours, I suggest you take some and move them into the category of enjoyable things to do. Like riding your bike.

Consider my own situation. Door to door, it takes me 30 minutes to get to my downtown office by car, assuming I can find a place to park it. The underground takes twenty minutes, but getting to and from the station, and waiting for it to

In the California city of Palo Alto, so many commuters bike to work, that special provisions, ranging from bike parking facilities to bicycle bridges, have been provided. Of course, the weather helps too.

Don't be deterred if your community isn't such a bicycling haven: though it is nice to have them, you can commute by bike remarkably well without such special provisions.

show up, adds another twenty. Or I can take my bike. Ride out there in thirty minutes and take my bike up into safety, just when I would be starting my search for a parking place if I took the car or elbowed my way to a vacant seat if I went on the underground.

My neighbor likes to ride his bike too. He has a $ 2000 bike and all the gadgets. Drives his car to work and back. About once a month, he puts the bike on a rack on the top of the car and drives out into the country somewhere to ride the bike, and his stomach testifies to the fact that he doesn't get much exercise that way. No time.

I don't have unlimited time either, yet I get to ride 5000 miles a year without even trying very hard. Call me fit, fitter than my neighbor anyway. Fit like me are another growing number of cyclists who don't wait until they get home from work to exercise, those who do as I do: ride their bike to work. This way, exercising does not have to be added to an otherwise unhealthy routine. Fitness and enjoyable cycling are natural to those who ride their bikes to work. With the added bonus that their minds have adapted to a healthy routine.

Sure enough, the urban jungle is not necessarily the most romantic environment to ride a bike. But many people live and work outside the inner cities. Even if you don't, have you ever wondered where this lush green heaven is where the healthy looking folk who are featured in the advertisements for bikes and accessories (and recently even in ads and commercials for items ranging from chewing gum to cigarettes) ride in pursuit of fitness? In real life they finish up riding on the same roads where we travel. They encounter about as much traffic as we do, and their accident rates are not lower but higher than ours. Because we bicycle commuters have learned to handle our bikes confidently

and expertly. It's not hard, you can learn to do it too, as I will show in this book.

## Mixed Transportation

It is not always possible, or desirable, to cycle to work — or wherever you are going — all the way and back. In many cases, combining the use of the bike with public transportation or carpooling makes more sense. Study the transportation options open to you and talk to others if it means carpooling. Often enough, your colleagues don't insist you take your turn driving, as long as you pay your share.

If you don't equip your bike too elaborately with racks and fenders, it will generally fit the trunk of most cars — or you can offer to provide a rack for that purpose. In some areas the public transportation authorities provide bike storage boxes that can be rented. In other cases you are taking a bit of a risk leaving your bike at a station or a bus stop. But you may find a store or a garage nearby where they will allow you to store your bike daily, either for pay or for love.

## The Bike for Other Uses

Once you have chosen to commute to work, your next choice can be made each day. Does today's trip justify taking the car, or would you rather ride the bike? By and by, you will discover that you can handle — and enjoy — more kinds of trips and more kinds of weather on the bike as you go on. I even go to the theater or the opera on my bike, but you don't have to: it's up to you, just as it is up to you whether you go there at all, or rather somewhere else. The bike is flexible enough, if you are.

But surely, you can't go shopping on the bike? Yes, you can: there are excellent bike racks and matching bags and other luggage carrying facilities available, and you can make some very handy items yourself. Some people go bike touring with 50 pounds of luggage — I don't, because I have learned to equip myself lighter, even when I go camping. But you can carry 40 pounds of groceries or other goodies a few miles on the bike without any hindrance. It's no punishment, it's convenient. Once again: you don't have to do it, but the choice is wide open to you.

## About this book

This book is divided into three distinct parts and an Appendix. In the first part, you will get familiar with the equipment. That includes the bike with its various components, luggage carrying gear, clothing and other accessories. In the second part, you will learn to become expert at handling the bike for general riding: chapters are devoted to adjusting the bike, health and safety, gearing and the various handling techniques. The third part addresses more extensively the specific situations that are typical in commuting, including urban traffic and cycling for transportation under a variety of conditions, and bicycle politics. The

Appendix, finally, contains tables for easy reference, including frame sizing and gearing tables.

The maintenance information included here does not compare with that contained in a full repair manual, since I assume that's not the reason you bought this book. To find out more about bicycle maintenance and repairs, you are referred to some of my other books, such as the *Bicycle Repair Book* or *Mountain Bike Maintenance*.

## Start Right Here

Before you've waded your way through these pages, there is no need to refrain from riding your bike. If you don't feel quite up to the trip to work, you may start cycling around the neighborhood, slowly adding trips to the store or the library and some other utilitarian cycling for the time being.

Get yourself a sturdy rack and a bag to carry some luggage on the bike. Carry or install lighting equipment, so you don't get stuck after dark, and a lock to make sure you don't lose your machine. Buy a good detailed map of the im-

Bicyling in London. As in big cities elsewhere, more and more people are finding out that the bicycle is a perfect means for getting around in this big, congested city. Recent public transport strikes have helped this trend along.

Properly equipped, the bike will carry everything you need. (Ben Swets photo)

mediate area, and start using your bike for it's original purpose: to get you around fast and conveniently.

Get to know your neighborhood, scout out some of the various roads that you can take. Perhaps you want to mark the map with some particular information about the points to reach and the suitability of various roads. Ride your bike to the store, the library, the tennis court, the post office. But don't stop there: you can ride the bike to visit friends, to the theater, to a restaurant or to church.

If you can't see yourself doing the latter, consider that you don't always have to ride around like a full-fledged bike racer. I usually ride to places like that in a conservative looking suit, and keep it looking fresh by not exerting myself on those trips quite so much that I perspire wildly. You'll find out there are an astonishing number of trips that lend themselves to bicycle use. Once you have grown accustomed to riding the bike naturally to get around, and as you learn more and more about the right way to go about it, you will find yourself leading a new life. A life where bicycle commuting seems natural. If bicycling is fun, than being a competent bicycle commuter is bliss. I promise you'll enjoy it.

# 2. Selecting a Commuting Bike

Though there are quite a number of different bicycles on the market today, not all of which are equally suitable for commuting and urban transportation, all have much in common. Before I shall show you how to go about selecting the best bike for your specific purpose, I will introduce the bicycle and its components in general terms.

**Parts of the Bicycle**

Fig. 2.1 illustrates the most important parts of any bicycle. Although a typical racing bike is illustrated, virtually all parts shown will be found on all other bicycles too, even though they may look different in some details.

The smartest way to look at your bike is by considering the various functional groups, which each comprise several related components. Thus, I like to consider the following functional groups of bicycle components and systems:

* the frame;
* the steering system;
* saddle and seatpost;
* the wheels;
* the drivetrain;
* the gearing system;
* the brakes;
* accessories.

In the sections that follow, I shall briefly describe each of these component groups.

*The Frame*

The frame can be considered the bicycle's backbone. It is the tubular structure to which all the other components are attached. Full details of the frame, together with information about the steering system and the saddle, will be found in Chapter 3.

*The Steering System*

The bicycle is not only steered, but also balanced, by means of the steering system. This assembly comprises the front fork, in which the front wheel is installed and which is pivoted in the front of the frame, as well as the handlebars with the stem that connects them to the fork, and

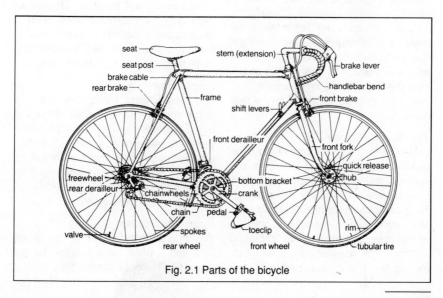

Fig. 2.1 Parts of the bicycle

the headset bearings which allow this assembly to turn relative to the frame.

### Saddle and Seatpost
The bike's seat, or saddle, is mounted on a tubular section called seatpost. The height of the saddle is adjusted by lowering or raising the seatpost, as it is clamped in the frame's seat tube. The angle and forward position of the saddle are also adjustable: by means of an adjustment mechanism integrated in the top of the seat post.

### The Wheels
Perhaps the biggest difference between the various types of bicycles is in the wheels: skinny, light ones for racing bikes, fat chunky ones for mountain bikes, heavy ones for utility bikes, small ones for folders and some other less common types. Each wheel consists of a central hub that rotates on ball bearings around the axle mounted in the frame, a rim with a tire mounted on it, and finally a network of spokes that connects the rim to the hub.

### The Drivetrain
The set of components that transmits the rider's effort to the rear wheel is referred to as the drivetrain. These parts include the bottom bracket in which the crank spindle rotates on ball bearings, the cranks with the chainrings mounted on the RH one, the pedals, the chain, and the freewheel mechanism with sprockets, or cogs, mounted on the rear wheel hub.

### The Gearing System
On virtually all bicycles used today, the gearing, used to adjust the ratio between pedaling speed and riding speed, is taken care of by means of derailleurs. These mechanisms are operated from shift levers and move the chain onto the appropriate combination of chainring and sprocket. Alternatively, some commuting bikes are equipped with hub gearing, comprising a mechanism enclosed in the rear wheel hub with anything from two to five gears.

### The Brakes
Operated by hand levers via flexible bowden cables, the brakes on virtually all modern bicycles squeeze together against the sides of the wheel rims to stop or slow down the wheels and the bike. Here too, alternatives exist for commuting use in the form of drum brakes built into the hubs of front and rear wheel.

### Accessories
Mostly, American bikes are devoid of accessories. A few are essential for any commuting purpose: pump, lock and luggage rack (or at least a bag). Certainly when riding in the rainy and dark season, fenders (or mud guards) and lighting equipment are recommended. Others may be useful, such as water bottle and speedometer (usually referred to as bicycle computer)

## Bicycle Types
Here is a brief summary of the most common bicycle types that lend themselves well to our purpose. Though almost any bike can be used after a fashion, only a limited number of models seems to be in favor with bicycle commuters and will be discussed here.

### Racing Bike
The thoroughbred racing bike is a light and rather fragile machine. Shown in Fig. 2.2, it usually has 12- or 14-speed derailleur gearing, very narrow tires and dropped handlebars. It generally weighs in at less than 23 lbs and lends itself for commuting only on very smoothly asphalted roads in fine weather.

### Sports or Triathlon Bike
This is a simpler version of the racing bike that is often more suitable for our purpose. Hard to distinguish at first

sight, it is generally made with slightly less sophisticated parts and often has more wide-range gearing and a less rigid geometry. The weight is perhaps two lbs more than a real racing bike of the same size.

### Mountain Bike
Shown in Fig. 2.3, this is the most popular bike sold these days. Originally intended for off-road use, it is also used to advantage on regular roads and city streets. Its thick tires, flat handlebars, powerful brakes and wide-range gearing make it an excellent choice for people who don't feel immediately at ease on a racing or sports bike. The weight is usually around 27—30 lbs. Don't overlook the off-road option, since riding off-road can sometimes get you to your goal quite efficiently, when the paved roads go a long way around and a short-cut will get you there more directly.

### Hybrid
Take a mountain bike and install slightly lighter tires, less extremely wide-range gearing and equip it for mixed use: you have a hybrid. Quite a nice bike for city use and also very suitable for all less confident riders. Typical weight 26—28 lbs.

### Touring Bike
At first glance, a touring bike, shown in Fig. 2.4, looks like a racing bike with luggage racks and sometimes fenders. There are more differences: heavier gauge frame tubes and other components, more generous clearances, wider tires, the kind of brakes used on a mountain bike and wide-range gearing. These bikes typically weigh about 27—30 lbs fully equipped.

### Other Models
Yes, though you'll rarely see them used these days, there are other bikes as well. They range from heavy utility bikes

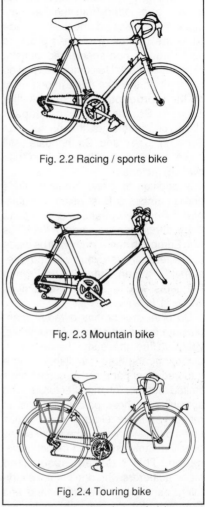

Fig. 2.2 Racing / sports bike

Fig. 2.3 Mountain bike

Fig. 2.4 Touring bike

to three-speeds, from folders to recliners, from tricycles and replicas of ancient machines to futuristic enclosed pedal-driven space capsules. Interesting, but mostly less practical for everyday use.

## Bicycle and Component Manufacturers
Most bicycles sold these days are made by major manufacturers. Although there still is a domestic bicycle industry in the US, the vast majority of quality bikes

sold through the specialized bicycle trade are imported from the Far East these days. Most domestically made bikes are the low end mass products sold through non-specialized outlets. Even those major US companies that do sell through the bike trade import most of their products from places like Taiwan, South Korea and Japan. However, several of these, such as Schwinn, Trek and Cannondale, still make their high-quality models in their own US factories.

In addition to these American firms and a number of East Asian manufacturers, the Europeans are not quite dead, although even some of the bikes with European names may well be made elsewhere. Thus, you will find presumably Italian Bianchis or French Peugeots with a sticker proclaiming, 'Made in Taiwan'.

On bikes from many different manufacturers, even custom-built machines, you will find the same frame tubes, brakes, gears, tires, handlebars and a hundred other parts that all come from a limited number of manufacturers who specialize in those particular items. In recent years the *'Gruppo'* concept has taken over, in which all the accessories bear the same brand and model designation. This has sent specialized manufactuerers who don't make everything, as the big ones (Shimano and Campagnolo) do, scrambling to find suppliers for the missing items. Thus, SunTour and numerous European firms buy certain components from other suppliers, though they are marked with their names and model designations.

Not all parts supplied by the same firm are of the same quality. A maker of brakes, for instance, may have half a dozen or more different models, ranging in price, type, size and quality from one end of the spectrum to the other. It will be impossible to give you very detailed

information indicating which make and model of any part will be better than other ones, if only because manufacturers change their product specifications and designations from time to time. Instead, I shall explain what to look for to make sure you are getting a satisfactory product for commuting purposes.

The thing to check is the ultimate functionality on the finished bike. For commuting, ruggedness is more important than lightness. If you mount the same model brake used on a fine racing bike on a commuting bicycle, or even on a typical sports bike that looks deceptively much like the racing machine, you may find that it does not even clear the tires, let alone provide good braking. When buying a complete bike, you should try out all the various components as they work on that particular machine. When replacing any components, make sure to take the bicycle on which they must be installed, or at a minimum the matching parts, to the bike store. This way the sales person or mechanic can help you select an item that is really satisfactory for your specific application.

### Size

Whether for commuting or any other purpose, it's important to buy a bike that is of the right size. The size is normally measured as the length of the seat tube. Some manufacturers measure this length from the center of the bottom bracket to the top of the seat lug, others to the center of the top tube (see Fig. 2.6). Table 1 in the Appendix gives the right size as a function of your leg length.

But the easiest way to establish the correct size for your use is to go to a bike shop and straddle the top tube of a number of bikes of the type you have in mind. With the feet flat on the ground, there should be some clearance above the top tube. Certainly if you are particularly

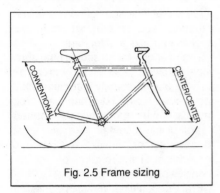

Fig. 2.5 Frame sizing

small, it may be hard to find a bike to fit comfortably. Keep in mind that the more expensive bikes tend to be made in the widest range of sizes. Furthermore, mountain bikes tend to be available in smaller sizes than racing bikes and touring machines.

## Women's Bikes

Many women have particular difficulties getting a bike to fit them properly. That is due to the manufacturers' desire to standardize. They provide off-the-peg frames to fit the averagely proportioned male. However, the typical woman has different proportions that don't match this standard scheme (see Fig. 2.6).

The woman's legs tend to be longer in relation to trunks and arms. Her arms are generally weaker and the hips heavier. In addition, women tend to be shorter (of course, short men may have as much trouble finding a properly proportioned bike). At least one female American manufacturer, Georgina Terry, offers a special series of bikes that are right for the averagely proportioned woman, based on a design pioneered by frame builder Bill Boston. Very fine machines that are available in many of the more sophisticated bike shops around the country. In addition, some of the major manufacturers now produce similar bikes for women, though they are still not as readily avail-

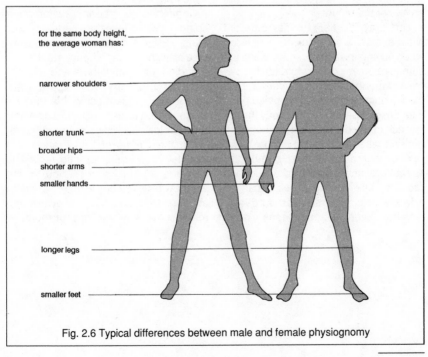

for the same body height, the average woman has:

narrower shoulders

shorter trunk
broader hips
shorter arms
smaller hands

longer legs

smaller feet

Fig. 2.6 Typical differences between male and female physiognomy

able as women's special needs would justify.

## Specific Commuting Needs

Yes, you can use almost any of the bikes listed in the first part of this chapter for commuting. And if you already have a bike, that will be the one to use. Just the same, a few points should be kept in mind if you buy a new bike with commuting in mind. These factors will be covered here.

A commuting bike should roll on sturdy wheels with tires that can stand some abuse. The recent trend towards mountain bikes and hybrids is certainly to the advantage of the bicycle commuter. On the other hand, racing and sports bikes — for those who prefer the dropped handlebar configuration — are actually becoming less readily available in versions with strong wheels and heavy-duty tires. And, sadly, the touring bike, which used to be a superb commuting alternative, has disappeared with the advent of the mountain bike.

You may be able to get different wheels, saddle or handlebars installed when buying the bike. This is always the time to express your preference for certain components anyway: whereas it becomes quite expensive to replace parts later on, you will only have to pay the difference in price if you select other components when first buying the bike.

Your commuting bike should be suitable for the installation of luggage rack, fenders and lights, so it can be adapted for any season and any weather. Generally, that means a more rugged machine with generous wheel clearance and brazed-on bosses and eyelets for racks and fenders.

The gearing system should offer such widely-spaced gears as are appropriate for your use. Generally that means that the typical racing bike had better be modified with more widely spaced gears, or the mountain bike with more modestly spaced ones. See Chapter 8 for additional information on the intricacies of derailleur gearing.

Brakes should be easy to operate. For the beginning cyclist that points to the mountain bike or the hybrid: the flat handlebars with immediately accessible brake levers allow you to concentrate on the road ahead without changing hand position when it comes time to apply the brakes. Similar considerations apply to the location of the gear shifters, which also seem to suggest the use of the mountain bike for all those cyclists who are not yet familiar with shifting a drop-handlebar bike.

Comfort is an important factor when riding a bike on less than perfect roads, as is often the case when commuting. One of my bikes has a heavy steel frame and ditto fork, handlebars and wheels. Though the inherent ruggedness seemed to suggest using this bike for commuting, it turned out to be a disaster: I almost lost the fillings out of my teeth riding the streets of San Francisco. I can't tell you whether a particular bike is comfortable, but I suggest you try out any new bike you buy with that factor in mind, taking it on a trial ride over rough roads, if that is typical for your route.

# 3. The Bicycle's Frame, Steering and Saddle

In the present chapter and the one that follows, you will be shown enough about your bike's major components to ride, handle and maintain the bike most effectively. Yes, you can ride without knowing all the technical ins and outs, but certainly for commuting use, it helps to be informed about the most general technical concepts. Here we will deal only with the bicycle's backbone: its frame with the steering system and saddle. In the next chapter we'll consider the many components installed on every bike, such as wheels, drivetrain, gears and brakes.

Of necessity, all this will involve some rather basic explanations and definitions of terminology, in addition to specific advice about bicycles and their components. Especially the former is required reading for those who are not fully familiar with the details of the bicycle. Others may be tempted to skip these chapters, assuming they contain nohing new.

Yet even these readers would do well to take this material to heart, since it contains quite a bit of information that will help you select bike and components and to spot what is wrong if your bike doesn't perform the way it should. Fur-

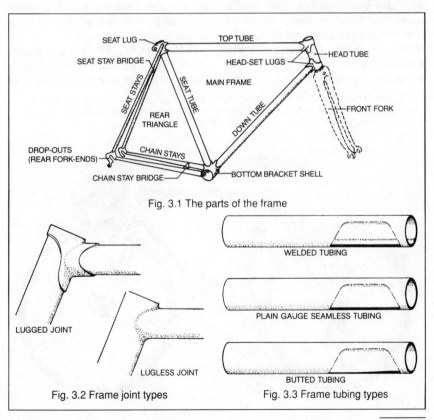

Fig. 3.1 The parts of the frame

Fig. 3.2 Frame joint types

Fig. 3.3 Frame tubing types

thermore, it will be helpful to at least check the illustrations and their labels, so you become familiar with the terms I shall be using to identify parts of the bike throughout the book. Often some of these things are called by different names in different parts of the world, and indeed by different people in the same area. Thus, confusion can only be avoided if we agree on the terminology that will be used elsewhere in this book.

## The Frame

The bicycle's frame, shown in Fig. 3.1, is its biggest single component. It consists of the main frame, built up of relatively large diameter tubes, and the rear triangle, consisting of double sets of tubes with smaller diameters. The main frame is made up of top tube, down tube, seat tube and head tube. The pairs of tubes that form the rear triangle are called seat stays and chain stays.

On most bikes, the large diameter tubes of the main frame are joined by means of parts referred to as lugs. The seat lug, which connects seat tube and top tube, is slotted in the back, allowing it to clamp around the saddle's seat post there. The lug that connects down tube and seat tube is called bottom bracket and accommodates the bearings for the crankset. The two forward lugs, connecting the head tube to down tube and top tube, respectively, are called head lugs and hold the bearings of the bike's steering system. Fig. 3.2 shows the difference between typical lugged and lugless frame joints.

The rear triangle's pairs of seat and chain stays each come together in flat plates, referred to as drop-outs or (rear) fork-ends, in which the rear wheel is installed. At the top, the seat stays are attached to the seat lug, while the chain stays run to the bottom bracket. The pairs of these stays are each stiffened by means of short transverse tubular bridge pieces.

The commuting bike's frame should preferably be equipped with several attachment lugs or bosses, referred to as

Superbly suitable for the bicycle commuter: the French *randonneur* bike, which was developed for touristic cycling. Unfortunately, virtually impossible to get readily equipped this way in the US.

braze-ons. These include items for the installation of accessories ranging from luggage racks to lights.

## Materials, Strength and Rigidity

Although some manufacturers offer very attractive bikes with frames made of aluminum alloy tubing, welded or bonded together with or without lugs, most bikes are still made with more traditional materials: various qualities of steel. On cheap bikes, the frame is made of simple carbon steel tubes that must have significant wall thicknesses (a minimum of 1.2 mm) to give adequate strength. This results in a rather heavy and 'dead' bike.

For more expensive machines that will be more comfortable to ride, strong steel alloys are used. These alloys contain small percentages of other materials, such as chrome, molybdenum and manganese. Generally, their strength is further increased through the tube forming operation. Due to these materials' greater inherent strength, the resulting frame is strong enough even when the tube wall thickness is much smaller. On most quality frames, the tubes have a greater wall thickness towards the ends (for adequate strength and resistance to the heat when joining the tubes) than elsewhere along the length of the tube, as shown in Fig. 3.3. The use of such tubes, referred to as butted tubes, results in a lighter, more responsive and comfortable bike.

Given adequate strength, the lighter bike is distinctly more enjoyable to ride, even if the difference seems minor relative to the total weight of bike and rider. This is due to the fact that, unlike the rider's own body weight, most of the weight of the bicycle (and any accessories and luggage the bike commuter carries) should be considered 'dead' weight or mass. Essentially, this is unsprung mass, which is not cushioned, as the equivalent weight of a car or motorcycle would be. Nor can it be transferred or shifted, as is the case for the rider's weight, which can be raised off the saddle in response to anticipated road shocks.

Another desirable feature, besides high strength and low weight, is adequate lateral and torsional rigidity of the bike. Rigidity means absence of flexibility. On a rigid bike, there is little deformation in response to a force applied to it at one point. Inadequate lateral and torsional rigidity leads to the propagation of vibrations, oscillations and swaying, particularly while riding fast on poor road surfaces or when changing direction abruptly. Unfortunately, rigidity is largely affected by some of the same factors as weight: for a given material and tube diameter, the rigidity decreases with decreasing wall

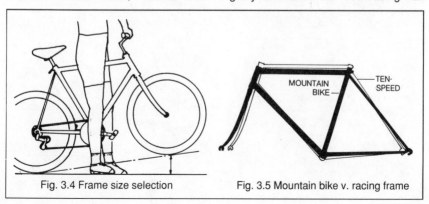

Fig. 3.4 Frame size selection          Fig. 3.5 Mountain bike v. racing frame

thickness. As long as you use the bike only for unloaded cycling on normal roads, there'll be no problem of flexing, but it becomes critical when riding hard on poorly surfaced roads or with luggage, where slightly heavier frames are in order.

The most effective way to achieve greater rigidity is to increase the diameter of the tubes. Whereas a 20% increase in wall thickness only leads to a proportional 20% increase in rigidity, the effect of a 20% greater outside diameter, even with an unchanged wall thickness, is on the order of 70%. Both methods lead to the same 20% weight increase. This is the reason why the frame's down and head tubes, which are most heavily subjected to torsional forces, are always made with a greater diameter than the other main tubes. It is also the reason most mountain bikes use bigger diameter frame tubes.

A third factor to keep in mind with regard to rigidity is the material used for the tubes. On the one hand, all types of steel, from the cheapest and weakest to the strongest and most exotic, have the same inherent rigidity (determined by a material property called modulus of elasticity). Consequently, given the same diameter and wall thickness, the tubes are equally rigid, whatever kind of steel is used. On the other hand, aluminum with all its alloys is considerably less rigid. Consequently, an aluminum frame should have tubes that have a greater wall thickness (required to compensate for this material's lower strength anyway), as well as a greater outside diameter, if it is to be satisfactory.

Only the conventional diamond shaped frame gives the required rigidity. That applies to bikes for men and for women alike, and all special women's models without a horizontal top tube are potentially dangerous at higher speeds, especially when loaded. Oddly enough, that applies particularly if the bike is made with high strength tubing, since it will have thinner walls.

Mountain bikes and hybrids, quite suitable for commuting, tend to have tubes of greater diameters, usually welded together without lugs. This makes them quite satisfactory, despite their generous dimensions. Aluminum frames must also have tubes of greater diameters, as well as a greater wall thickness. Since aluminum is so much

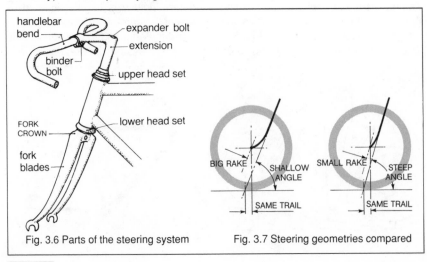

Fig. 3.6 Parts of the steering system          Fig. 3.7 Steering geometries compared

lighter than steel, the overall weight will still be quite low.

### Frame Dimensions

A bicycle's nominal size is determined by the frame size, which is defined as the length of the seat tube. Unfortunately, different manufacturers measure this dimension differently, as shown in Fig. 2.6 in Chapter 2. In the English speaking world, the distance between the center of the bottom bracket and the top of the seat lug used to be quoted. Lately, it is becoming more customary to follow the French method of measuring between the center of the bottom bracket and the center of the top tube. The same frame will be quoted as being 15 mm, or about $1/2$ inch, smaller in the latter case than in the former.

To select a frame of the right size, you can either use the advice contained in Table 1 in the Appendix, or you can try out some frames for fit. With wheels of the correct size installed, the top tube should be at such a height that you can straddle it with both feet flat on the ground, wearing thin-soled shoes with minimal heels (see Fig. 3.4). Most people seem to buy a bike that is too big. When in doubt, I would suggest you deviate on the smaller, rather than on the larger side.

A mountain bike may have slightly more generous dimensions and clearances, including shallower angles between the horizontal and the seat tube and steering axis, as shown in Fig. 3.5, but with a shorter seat tube (resulting in a lower top tube).

The commuting bike's frame should preferably be equipped with threaded bosses and lugs for the installation of accessories such as racks and fenders.

### The Steering System

This is the assembly of parts that keeps the bike on track and balanced, by allowing the rotational plane of the front wheel to pivot relative to the rest of the bike. As shown in Fig. 3.6, it comprises the fork, headset bearings, handlebar stem, or extension, and the handlebars.

### The Front Fork

The fork consists of two blades, terminating in fork-ends, or front drop-outs, a fork crown and a steerer tube, which is threaded at one end to accept the adjustable parts of the headset. The fork should be of similar materials to those used for a good frame: strong alloy tubing, brazed onto the fork crown and with relatively thick fork-ends.

Compared to a mountain bike or a touring machine, the racing or sports

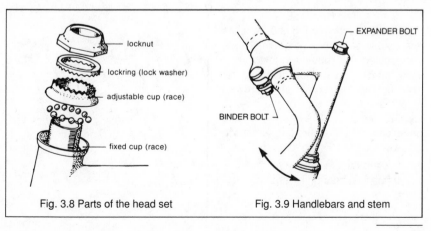

locknut
lockring (lock washer)
adjustable cup (race)
fixed cup (race)

EXPANDER BOLT
BINDER BOLT

Fig. 3.8 Parts of the head set          Fig. 3.9 Handlebars and stem

bike's fork has less off-set, or rake. This is necessary to achieve the same steering characteristics, as shown in Fig 3.7. Typical values for a racing bike are a steerer tube angle of 73—74 degrees and a rake of 45—55mm, as compared to 68—72 degrees and a rake of 60—65mm for a mountain bike, hybrids falling somewhere in between.

If the steerer tube angle is smaller, which provides a more cushioned ride and is desirable on rough roads, the fork rake should be correspondingly greater to achieve the same steering characteristics.

In a collision, the fork will generally be the most likely part to get damaged. Although such a bent fork can sometimes be straightened again, it will be smart to check with a bike mechanic, rather than experimenting around yourself. When in doubt, have a new fork installed.

The length of the fork's steerer tube is a function of the frame size. There are two distinct threading standards in use: French and English. The latter standard is used on most bikes. Nowadays even most frames made for export by French manufacturers are usually supplied with English threading. It will be a good idea to take the old fork and a matching threaded part of the headset along when replacing a bent fork.

### The Headset

The headset, shown in Fig. 3.8, consists of a double set of ball bearings. These are installed at the upper and lower ends of the head tube, with the matching parts fixed on the fork crown and screwed onto the threaded part of the steerer tube, respectively. The headset should be adjusted if the steering is either too loose or too tight. Proceed as follows:

**1.** Loosen the big locknut on the upper headset bearing by about 3—4 turns.

**2.** Unscrew the lock washer far enough to allow turning the bearing race immediately below.

**3.** Tighten or loosen the adjustable race as required, by turning it clockwise or counterclockwise, respectively.

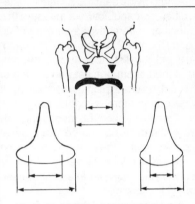

Fig. 3.10 Saddle width determination

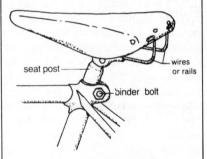

Fig. 3.11 Saddle and seat post

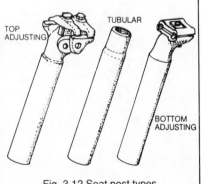

Fig. 3.12 Seat post types

**4.** Put the lock washer in place and tighten the locknut, while holding the adjustable race.

**5.** If problems persist, see a bike shop.

### Handlebars and Stem

The handlebars are attached to the fork's steerer tube by means of an L-shaped piece called handlebar stem. The lower end of this device fits inside the steerer tube. As shown in Fig. 3.9, a wedge or cone-shaped part can be pulled into the stem to clamp the two parts together by tightening the expander bolt. The latter is reached from the top and is generally operated by means of a hexagonal bar tool, referred to as Allan key. At least 65 mm (2.5 in) of the stem must remain contained inside the steerer tube for safety reasons.

The handlebar proper, also referred to as handlebar bend, is held in a split or otherwise clamped portion at the forward end of the stem. Here it is clamped by tightening a second bolt, referred to as binder bolt. Stems are generally made of aluminum alloy and are available in several different extension lengths. A different stem size may be necessary to adapt the distance between saddle and handlebars to the rider for maximum comfort, as will be described in Chapter 7.

Handlebar bends are generally made of aluminum tubing. They are available in several distinct shapes, ranging from the wide flat things installed on mountain bikes to the narrow and deep models used on pure racing machines. For commuting bikes, either model can be suitable, but beginning cyclists are generally better served with the type installed on mountain bikes or hybrids, providing they are relatively narrow.

The middle part of the handlebar bend must be reinforced by an interior or exterior reinforcing sleeve (resulting in a section of greater diameter) over a length of at least 5 cm (2 in) to eliminate the chance of breaking the bar at the point where it projects from the stem. Handlebar bend and stem must be matched, since handlebar diameters vary from one make and model to the other.

The dropped bar is finished off by wrapping cloth or plastic handlebar tape around it. Alternately, you may choose to install flexible foam plastic sleeves. The latter solution appears to be most comfortable for cycling on less than perfect road surfaces. The open ends of the dropped handlebar bend are closed off by plugs, while the flat bars of mountain bikes and hybrids have plastic hand grips.

### Saddle and Seat Post

Certainly if you are relatively new to cycling, the saddle, or seat, had better be comfortable. Most beginning cyclists prefer to sit more upright than is customary for bicycle racing. This results in more weight resting on the saddle and

The bicycle's 'front end': handlebars, headset and front fork

The bicycle saddle: if you adjust it correctly, it is quite comfortable

more difficulty lifting the weight to relieve pain. Consequently, a different saddle design may be required. In general, a good touring or mountain bike saddle will do the trick. This should be somewhat wider in the back, though still as long and narrow in the front as the racing saddle. In particular women, who usually have a wider pelvis then most men,

may need a wide, padded model. See Fig. 3.10 for seat width details.

Fig. 3.11 shows the way the saddle is attached to the frame at the seat lug by means of a seat post. The attachment bolts that hold the saddle to the seat post may be either on top, underneath or by the side of the seat clip that holds the saddle wires to the seat post.

The seat post should be of a model that allows fine adjustment of the position and the angle relative to the horizontal plane. Select one of the micro-adjustable models, as shown in Fig. 3.12. The seat post diameter should match the inside diameter of the seat tube, being 27.2 mm on most conventional quality frames built with butted tubing, 26.8 mm for most mountain bikes. The seat post is held at the right height by clamping the split seat lug around it when the seat binder bolt is tightened. The seat post should be so long that at least 65 mm (2.5 in) is held inside the seat lug for safety reasons. See Chapter 7 for saddle adjustments.

# 4. The Bicycle's Other Parts

In the present chapter, the bike's remaining components will be described in the same functional groups mentioned in Chapter 2: wheels, drivetrain, gearing system and brakes. Any accessories will be treated separately in Chapter 5. The gearing system, which is handled here summarily, will be covered more fully in Chapter 8.

Some elementary maintenance instructions are included here for the components discussed. This is only done in those cases where it seems relevant in the context of a book like this. When you get into trouble *en route* because you have a flat or the chain comes off, you'll want to know what to do about it. On the other hand, there are numerous other possible maintenance or repair jobs that are not relevant here. You can get full information from my *Bicycle Repair Book*, while the less ambitious may choose to take their machine to a bike store.

## The Wheels

A typical bicycle wheel is shown in Fig. 4.1. It is a spoked wheel with regular wired-on tires, which consist of a separate inner tube and a tire casing that is held tight in a deep bedded metal rim by means of metal-wire-reinforced beads. The other components of the wheel are hub and spokes. Wheel problems are perhaps the most common category of incidents, and their repair will be covered in some detail.

The hub, shown in Fig. 4.2, may be either a high flange or a low flange model. On most quality bikes the hubs have quick-release levers, allowing easy wheel removal (see Fig. 4.3).

The spokes, shown in Fig. 4.4, should be of stainless steel, and there are usually 36 of them per wheel. Each spoke is held to the rim by means of a screwed-on nipple. Theys should be kept tightened to maintain the spokes under tension, which keeps the wheel trued and prevents spoke breakage.

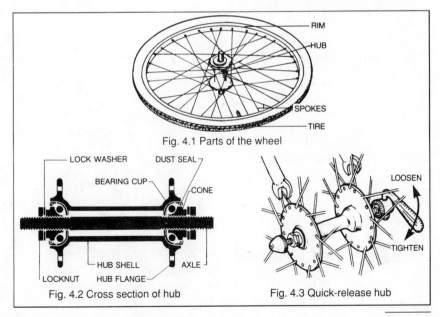

Fig. 4.1 Parts of the wheel

Fig. 4.2 Cross section of hub

Fig. 4.3 Quick-release hub

The spokes run from the hub to the rim in one of several distinct patterns. Fig. 4.5 shows three-cross and four-cross spoking patterns.

The length of the spoke is measured as shown in Fig. 4.4 and depends on the wheel size, the type of hub, and the spoking pattern. The thickness is usually 1.8 mm (or 15 gauge) on a sports or racing bike, 2.0 mm (14 gauge) on mountain bikes and hybrids. Butted spokes have a thinner section in the middle and are as strong as regular spokes that are as thick as their thickest section (the lower gauge number in their size designation). If a spoke should break, get it replaced as soon as possible.

### The Rims

For a commuting bike of any quality, the rims must be of aluminum. In addition to the weight advantage, aluminum provides much better wet weather braking than chrome plated steel rims. Fig. 4.6 illustrates the rim with a tire installed.

The spoke holes should be reinforced by means of ferrules. To protect the tube, a strip of rim tape should cover the part of the rim bed where the spoke nipples would otherwise touch the inner tube.

### Wheel Truing

If the wheel is bent, proceed as follows to straighten it by retensioning certain spokes, as shown in Fig. 4.7:

**1.** Check just where it is off-set to the left, where to the right, by turning it slowly while watching at a fixed refe-

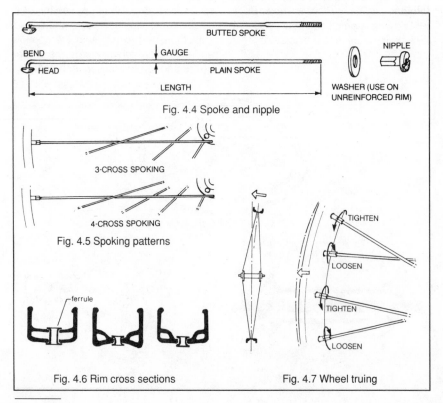

Fig. 4.4 Spoke and nipple

Fig. 4.5 Spoking patterns

Fig. 4.6 Rim cross sections

Fig. 4.7 Wheel truing

rence point, such as the brake shoes. Mark the relevant sections.

**2.** In the area where the rim is off-set, loosen the spokes leading to the hub flange on that same side, while tightening those lthat lead to the hub flange on the opposite side.

**3.** Repeat steps 1 and 2 until the wheel is true enough not to rub on the brakes.

This will get you to work and back. However, unless you are quite good at it, I suggest you get the job done properly by a bike mechanic as soon as possible.

### Tires and Tubes

The size of the tire defines the nominal size of the wheel (see Fig. 4.8). Adult sports and racing bikes usually have either 27 in or 700 mm tires of a rather narrow section. The nominal sizes are a far cry from their actual dimensions: the supposed 700 mm tires normally measure anywhere from 666 mm to 686 mm, depending on their width. Though these things are also known as 28 in

tires, they are actually smaller than those of nominal size 27 in.

The inner tube should be of a size to match the tire. For any given size, it seems the lighter and thinner tube and tire give a better ride. Only in terrain with thorns and other frequent puncture causes, should the very thick thorn-proof tubes be used.

Tire and rim must match. The critical dimension determining tire interchangeability is the rim bed, or rim shoulder, dimension. For 27 in and 700 mm tires this diameter should be 630 mm and 622 mm, respectively. Mountain bikes that roll on 26 in tires have rims of 559 mm rim bed diameter, while hybrid bikes typically have 622 mm rims.

As for the recommended tire width, it all depends on the terrain encountered. The minimum width suitable for use on good roads is probably 22 mm, while 25, 28 or even 32 mm are good choices for commuting use on mixed road surfaces. If you want to ride off-road or in regions where roads are maintained less scrupulously, hybrids and mountain bikes with tire widths anywhere from 35

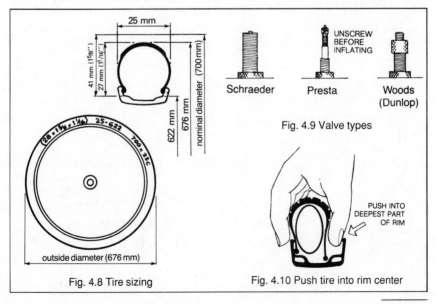

Fig. 4.8 Tire sizing

Fig. 4.9 Valve types

Fig. 4.10 Push tire into rim center

mm to 54 mm are an excellent choice. Always look for a model with flexible sidewalls, which roll significantly lighter, especially on rough surfaces.

The tube is inflated by means of a valve, several types of which are illustrated in Fig. 4.9. By far the most suitable is the Presta valve, which requires much less force to inflate, though it can't be done by means of a gas station air hose. Unscrew the round nut at the tip before inflating, and tighten it again afterwards. Inflation pressure is the key to low rolling resistance and immunity to puncturing. Maintain at least the pressure quoted on the tire side wall, and don't hesitate to inflate at least the one in the rear by about 20 percent more than that minimum value.

### Fixing a Flat

Sooner or later every bicycle commuter gets a flat. It helps if you are able to handle this repair yourself, so you may be a few minutes late for work, but not at a loss. Carry a tire patch kit, three tire irons, a pump and perhaps a spare tube. The adhesive quality of the patches in your kit deteriorates over time, so I sug-

gest replacing them once a year. Proceed as follows:

**1.** Remove the wheel from the bike. On a rear wheel, first select the gear with the small chainwheel and the smallest sprocket, then hold the chain with the derailleur back.

**2.** Check whether the cause is visible from the outside. In that case, remove it and mark the location, so you know where to work.

**3.** Remove the valve cap and locknut, unscrew the round nut (if you have a Presta valve).

**4.** Push the valve body in and work one side of the tire into the deeper center of the rim, as shown in Fig. 4.10.

**5.** Put a tire iron under the bead on that side, about six inches from the valve, then use it to lift the bead over the rim edge and hook it on a spoke, as shown in Fig. 4.11.

**6.** Do the same with the second tire iron two or three spokes to the left, and with the third over to the right. Now the first one will come loose, so you may use it in a fourth location, if necessary.

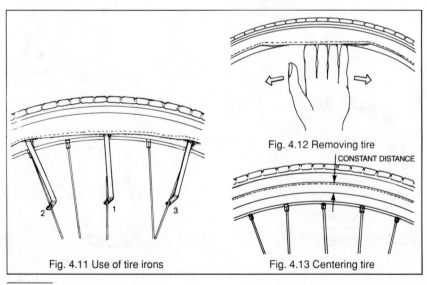

Fig. 4.11 Use of tire irons

Fig. 4.12 Removing tire

Fig. 4.13 Centering tire

**7.** When enough of the tire sidewall is lifted over the rim, you can lift the rest over by hand (see Fig. 4.12).

**8.** Remove the tube, saving the valve until last; push the valve out through the valve hole.

**9.** Try inflating, and check where air escapes. If the hole is very small, so it can't be easily detected, pass the tube slowly past your eye, which is quite sensitive. If still no luck, dip the tube under water, a section at a time: the hole is wherever bubbles escape. Mark its location and dry the tire if appropriate. There may be more than just one hole.

**10.** Make sure the area around the hole is dry and clean, then roughen it with the sand paper or the scraper from the patch kit, and remove the resulting dust. Treat an area slightly larger than the patch you want to use.

**11.** Quickly spread a thin, even film of rubber solution on the treated area. Let dry about 3 minutes.

**12.** Remove the foil backing from the patch, without touching the adhesive surface. Place it with the adhesive side down on the treated area, centered on the hole. Apply pressure over the entire patch to improve adhesion.

**13.** Sprinkle talcum powder from the patch kit over the treated area.

**14.** Inflate the tube and wait long enough to make sure the repair has been carried out properly.

**15.** Meanwhile, check the inside of the tire and remove any sharp objects that may have caused the puncture. Also make sure no spoke ends project from the rim bed — file flush if necessary and cover with rim tape.

**16.** Let enough air out of the tube to make it limp but not completely empty. Then reinsert it under the tire, starting at the valve.

**17.** Pull the tire back over the edge of the rim *with your bare hands*, working in both directions, starting opposite the valve, which must be done last of all. If it seems too tight, work the part al-

Component *'gruppo'* for medium-priced bicycles from Campagnolo

ready installed deeper into the center of the rim bed.

**18.** Make sure the tube is not pinched between rim and tire bead anywhere, working and kneading the tire until the tube is free.

**19.** Install the valve locknut and inflate the tube to about a third of its final pressure.

**20.** Center the tire relative to the rim, making sure it lies evenly all around on both sides (see Fig. 4.13).

**21.** Inflate to its final pressure, then install the wheel. If the tire is wider than the rim, you may have to release the brake (just make sure you tighten it again afterwards). On the rear wheel, refer to point 1 above.

**Note:** If the valve leaks, or if the tube is either porous or seriously damaged, the entire tube — when damaged, the casing — must be replaced, following the relevant steps of these instructions.

### The Drivetrain

The bicycle's drivetrain comprises the parts that transmit the power from the rider's legs to the rear wheel. The gearing system is often considered part of the drivetrain as well, but I prefer to treat it separately.

The heart of the drivetrain is the crankset, which is installed in the frame's bottom bracket. It turns around a spindle or axle that is supported in ball bearings. The two types of bottom bracket bearing systems used on quality bicycles are the adjustable cup-and-cone type and the non-adjustable cartridge type, usually incorrectly referred to as sealed bearing unit. These two varieties are depicted in Fig. 4.14 and Fig. 4.15, respectively.

On virtually all quality bikes built nowadays, the spindle has tapered square ends, matching correspondingly shaped holes in the cranks. The crank is held on the spindle by means of a bolt, covered by a dust cap in the crank. This method of attachment is referred to as cotterless and is shown in Fig. 4.16. Spindle lengths, bottom bracket widths, screw threading and taper shape all may vary, even if (different) models of the same make are installed. Consequent-

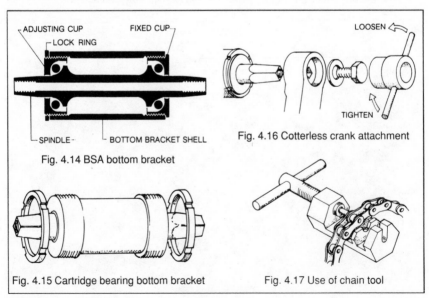

Fig. 4.14 BSA bottom bracket

Fig. 4.16 Cotterless crank attachment

Fig. 4.15 Cartridge bearing bottom bracket

Fig. 4.17 Use of chain tool

ly, all parts of the bottom bracket can only be replaced when the original part to be replaced and some matching part are taken along to the shop, to make sure they fit as a system.

The cranks are generally made of aluminum and are available in several different lengths. Unless you have particularly long or short legs, the standard size of 17 cm (about 7 in) will be quite satisfactory.

### Tighten Cotterless Crank

On a new bike, the cranks tend to come loose after some use, as they may at more infrequent intervals later on. For this reason, and for other maintenance or replacement work, I suggest you obtain a matching crank tool for the particular make and model installed on your bike. Check and tighten the cranks every 25 miles during the first 100 miles, and perhaps once a month afterwards.

**1.** Remove the dust cap with any fitting tool (on most models a coin may be used).

**2.** Using the wrench part of the special crank tool, tighten the re-

cessed bolt firmly, countering at the crank.

**3.** Reinstall the dust cap.

### Chainrings

The RH crank has an attachment spider for installation of the chainrings, also called chainwheels. Racing and sports bikes usually have two, while mountain bikes have three chainrings. Check the attachment bolts of the chainrings from time to time, and tighten them evenly if necessary.

Nowadays, most sports bikes, hybrids and mountain bikes are equipped with non-round chainrings, such as the popular Shimano Biopace. They are claimed to help inexperienced riders pedal more efficiently but have no advantage to anyone who has learned to pedal fast, as will be explained in Chapter 8.

### The Chain

The chain connects the crankset with the rear wheel, where a freewheel block with several different size sprockets, or cogs, is installed. The chain is routed as

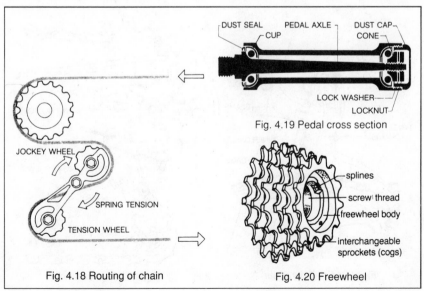

Fig. 4.19 Pedal cross section

Fig. 4.18 Routing of chain

Fig. 4.20 Freewheel

explained below. It must have the right length: it should neither hang loose nor tighten up excessively when using either of the extreme gearing combinations (biggest chainring with the biggest sprocket or smallest chainring with the smallest sprocket).

### Chain Removal and Installation

On derailleur bikes, an endless chain is used, which may be parted by removing one of the pins connecting two links. The same method is used to add or remove links to adjust the chain's length. It may be necessary to remove the chain for cleaning and lubrication. To do that, you will need a chain tool, which is used as illustrated in Fig. 4.17 and described below:

**1.** Put the chain on a combination of a small chainwheel with the smallest sprocket, to release its tension.

**2.** Place the tool on one of the pins connecting two links, and turn it in by 6 turns.

**3.** Turn the handle of the tool back out and remove the tool from the chain.

**4.** Wriggle the chain apart.

**5.** Reinstall the chain, routing it around the derailleur per Fig. 4.18.

### The Pedals

The pedals are installed at the ends of the cranks. Fig. 4.19 shows the guts of one. The threaded end is screwed in — the LH one with LH-thread, the RH one with normal RH-thread. On most lightweight bicycles, either toeclips are used to hold the feet to the pedals, or a special 'clipless' pedal with matching shoe.

### The Freewheel

Depending on the make and type of rear wheel hub, the freewheel is either screwed on, or it is a separate unit integrated in the (special) hub, referred to as cassette type. Though the latter, of which the Shimano Cassette Freehub is the best know, are quite satisfactory in use, their disadvantage is that the entire wheel has to be replaced (or at least rebuilt) if the freewheel mechanism fails. Fig. 4.20 shows a common screwed-on freewheel with its cogs.

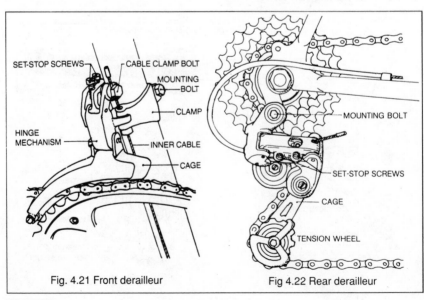

Fig. 4.21 Front derailleur          Fig 4.22 Rear derailleur

## The Gearing System

In this section we'll discuss only the hardware, while the niceties of the system, including selection and handling, are described in Chapter 8.

A typical derailleur system consists of a front derailleur, or changer, and a rear derailleur, which are operated by means of shift levers. The shifters may be installed either on the down tube, at the handlebar ends or, in the case of a bike with flat handlebars, on top of the bars. Other shift lever positions, such as at the handlebar stem, are inherently unsuitable, since they are not easily accessible without negatively affecting bike handling. The shifters are connected to the changers by means of flexible cables that run over guides and, in the case of handlebar-mounted shifters, partly inside flexible outer cables.

## The Derailleurs

The front changer, or front derailleur, shown in Fig. 4.21, is installed on the seat tube, either by means of a clip around the tube or by means of brazed-on lug. The rear derailleur, depicted in Fig. 4.22, is installed on the RH dropout, which should have a threaded eye for this purpose, though adaptor plates are provided with most derailleurs to allow installing them on a frame without. The chain is routed around the rear derailleur as shown in Fig. 4.18, while it is guided through the changer's cage in the front.

The derailleurs shift the chain over sideways to engage a smaller or bigger chainring or sprocket, while you continue to pedal forward with reduced pedal force. The combination of a large chainring and a small sprocket provides

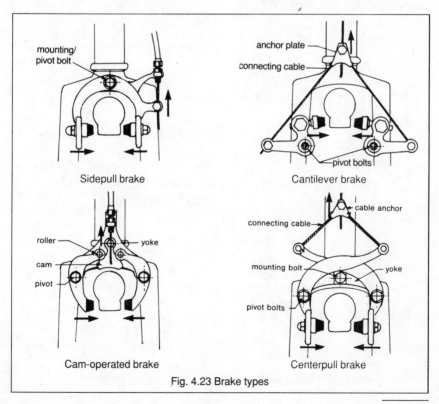

mounting/pivot bolt

Sidepull brake

anchor plate
connecting cable
pivot bolts

Cantilever brake

roller
cam
pivot
yoke

Cam-operated brake

cable anchor
connecting cable
mounting bolt
yoke
pivot bolts

Centerpull brake

Fig. 4.23 Brake types

a high gear, suitable for easy terrain conditions. Engaging a small chainring and a large sprocket provides a low gear, required for going up an incline, starting off or riding against a head wind. See Chapter 8 for further details, including adjustment, which is often necessary to stop the chain from being 'dumped' when shifting.

### The Brakes

There are four different types of rim brakes in use for commuting bikes. Fig. 4.23 shows the various types, referred to as centerpull, sidepull, cantilever, and cam-operated brakes, respectively.

On the sidepull brake, the brake arms pivot around the attachment bolt. They pivot around separate bosses installed on a common yoke on the centerpull brake. On the cantilever brake and the frame-mounted version of the centerpull (referred to as U- brake) as well as the cam-operated brake, the pivots are installed on bosses that are attached directly to the fork (in the front) and the seat or chain stays (in the rear).

The force applied by pulling the lever is transmitted to the brake unit by means of flexible cables. These cables are partly contained in flexible outer cables and restrained at anchor points on the frame.

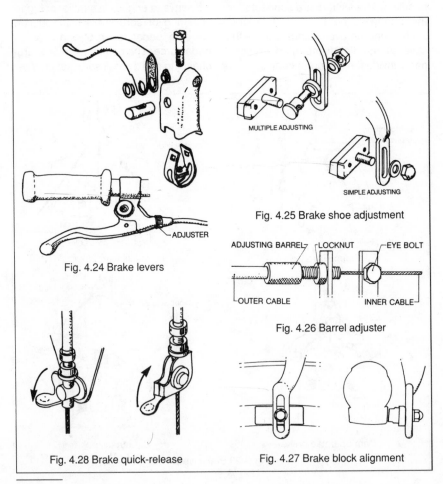

Fig. 4.24 Brake levels

MULTIPLE ADJUSTING

SIMPLE ADJUSTING

Fig. 4.25 Brake shoe adjustment

ADJUSTING BARREL  LOCKNUT   EYE BOLT

OUTER CABLE   INNER CABLE

Fig. 4.26 Barrel adjuster

Fig. 4.28 Brake quick-release

Fig. 4.27 Brake block alignment

The force is transmitted to the parts of the brake unit to which the cable is attached. A pivoting action then pulls the ends of the brake arms with the brake blocks against the sides of the rim to create the drag that slows down the bike.

On most sports and racing bikes, sidepull brakes are installed, while cantilevers, cam-operated brakes and U-brakes are used on mountain bikes, hybrids and touring machines.

Some i nteresting new brake designs that seem suitable for commuting bikes have resecntly been introduced. One of these is the hydraulic brake offered in an affordable version by Magura. Two other European manufacturers, Sachs-Huret and Sturmey-Archer, offer superb drum brakes, while several Japanese manufacturers offer disk brakes.

### Brake Levers

The brake lever, examples of which are shown in Fig. 4.24, should match the handlebar type used and it should be easy to reach, while allowing full application of the brake. The type of lever designed for mountain bikes is quite suitable for any bike with flat handlebars, providing the attachment clamp matches the bar diameter. For drop handlebars, models with extension levers are not satisfactory, even for beginners, since they are insufficiently rigid and often shorten the regular handle's range of travel.

### Brake Blocks

The brake blocks should preferably be of a composition material that provides adequate braking even in the rain, which is just not the case with any kind of plain rubber brake blocks. Depending on the type of brake used, the brake blocks may be installed in one of the two basic types of brake shoes illustrated in Fig. 4.25, which are adjustable in one and two planes, respectively.

Contrary to popular belief, longer brake blocks are not better but, if anything, poorer than shorter ones, given the same material. This is due to the lower per-unit pressure resulting from the same lever force, which reduces the shorter longer brake block's ability to squeeze water from the rim when it is wet.

### Brake Test

To make sure the brakes work properly, try them out separately at walking speed, which is perfectly safe and still gives a representative test of the deceleration reached with each brake. Used alone while riding the bike, the rear

SunTour components for mountain bikes and hybrids. Note the combined brake levers and gear shifters. Especially for less experienced cyclists in urban traffic, such readily accessible levers are particularly safe and convenient.

brake must be strong enough to skid the wheel when applied firmly. The front brake should decelerate the bike so much that the rider notices the rear wheel lifting off when it is applied fully. If their performance is inadequate, carry out the adjustment described below.

## Adjust Brakes

We will assume the brake must be adjusted because its performance is insufficient. In this case, the cable tension must be increased by decreasing its length. Should the brake touch the rim even when not engaged, the opposite must be done. The adjuster mechanism is shown in Fig. 4.26.

Before starting, check to make sure the brake blocks lie on the rim properly over their entire width and length when the brake is applied, as shown in Fig. 4.27. Ideally, the front of the brake block should touch the rim just a little earlier than the back. If necessary, adjust by loosening the brake block bolt, moving the block as appropriate. Retighten it while holding the brake block in the right position. The brake blocks may be replaced if they are worn down significantly, after which the follogin adjustment must be carried out as well.

*Adjusting procedure*

**1.** Release brake quick-release (see Fig. 4.28).

**2.** Loosen locknut on the adjusting mechanism.

**3.** While holding the locknut, screw the barrel adjuster out by several turns; then tighten the quick-release again.

**4.** Check the brake tension: the brake must grab the rim firmly when a minimum of 2 cm ($^3/4$ in) clearance remains between the brake handle and the handlebars.

**5.** If necessary, repeat steps 1—4 until the brake works properly.

**6.** Tighten the locknut again, while holding the adjusting barrel to stop it from turning.

# 5. Accessories and Other Equipment

In this chapter we shall examine the accessories that can be hung on the bike and the various other items that may be handy for bicycle commuting. Some of the equipment described here is intended for specific uses and not necessarily recommended for use by every cyclist all the time. Just the same, it will be useful to know what is available and how to select the right accessories either now or later.

In order to install accessories on a bicycle without special provisions such as eyelets and threaded bosses, you have to rely on provisional clamps and the like. It will be advisable to attach any such clamps only after installing a rubber patch from the bicycle tire patch kit around the bike's tubing locally (Fig. 5.1). This not only protects paintwork or metal finish, it also prevents the clamp from slipping or twisting. Do not use self-adhesive tape for this purpose, since it will slip over time, whereas a tire patch, applied just like you would do to fix a flat tire, will stay in place firmly.

By way of maintenance of most accessories, you merely have to make sure the things are not broken or loose. Tighten the various attachment bolts from time to time, preferably on a regular basis. To make sure bolts do not come loose, I suggest you use washers and locknuts wherever possible.

### Bags and Racks

For most commuting purposes, you will want to be able to carry things on the bike, even if it is only a rain cape or your briefcase. And that is best done with the use of racks, though some bags are available that attach directly to the bike. Either way is preferable to carrying

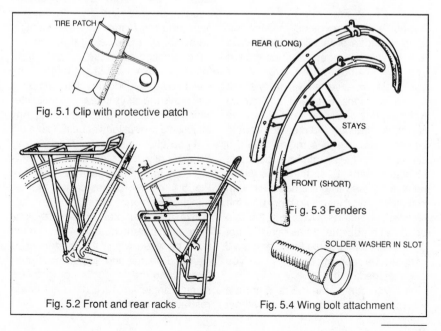

Fig. 5.1 Clip with protective patch

Fig. 5.2 Front and rear racks

Fig. 5.3 Fenders

Fig. 5.4 Wing bolt attachment

things in a backpack, which hinders you while cycling.

Luggage racks, shown in Fig. 5.12) are available for the front and the rear. Generally, the rear rack allows carrying relatively large bags by the side and on top, while the one in the front is smaller, being attached to the fork. Interesting only when you have to carry a lot of luggage.

Whatever their type, make sure the racks can be attached very firmly to the bike. Preferably, brazed-on attachment lugs or bosses should be installed on the bike, exactly matching the dimensions of the particular rack used. That may become a bit of a problem when replacing the rack on a used bike or when installing one on a bike for the first time. However, a certain degree of standardization has taken place. Most manufacturers design their equipment in line with the attachment details of the racks produced by Jim Blackburn. Special versions of these are available for mountain bikes.

### Fenders

Although many cyclists in America abhor the idea of installing fenders on their bicycle, I suggest you use them if you are serious about cycling for transportation — certainly in rainy areas or rainy seasons. Even if it isn't raining while you ride, the spray from a wet road is just as irritating. You may not want to bother if you live in a region where it simply doesn't ever rain for a period of several months. Even then, you would be well advised to get fenders, though you may hold off installing them until the rainy season starts. Cycling in the rain or on wet roads after it has rained is not as bad as some people think, and it will certainly be less miserable when you are equipped for it.

Yes, you can ride in the rain, or on a wet road after the rain, on a bike without fenders. But you'll be dead miserable. A spray of muddy water will stain your back and your bike; another jet of water will be shooting at your feet, and there's no way to get comfortable that way. You'll be in a lousy mood when you make it to the office and you'll look even worse. Though you may still need rain gear to keep the rain off the top, you'll find fenders at least keep you reasonably dry and clean from below.

Fig. 5.3 shows typical fenders. At the top, they are attached to the brake bolt behind the front fork and in front of the bridge connecting the seat stays, for front and rear fenders, respectively. In the rear, a second point of attachment is by means of a clip over the bridge just behind the bottom bracket. Finally, they are held by means of rather thin stays to the front fork-ends and rear drop-outs, respectively.

Install plain washers between bolts or nuts and the various clips or stays. The fender should be mounted in such a way that about 12 mm ($^1/2$ in) radial and at least 6 mm ($^1/4$ in) lateral clearance remains between the tires on the one hand and the fender with its mounting hardware on the other. If the fender is either crooked, too close, or too far from the wheel, do not adjust it by bending the stays. Instead, undo the clamping point and move the stays in or out to suit, after which the bolt is tightened again. Any excessive protrusions should be cut off.

If you choose to install fenders only occasionally, removable attachments are easy enough to make, as shown in Fig. 5.4. If the bike has caliper brakes, attached by means of single bolts in fork crown and rear brake bridge, replace their attachment nuts by two thinner nuts, between which the fender clip is clamped. Install and tighten both nuts, even when the fender is not installed, since a single thin nut is not adequate to restrain the brake.

Fenders may be either of plastic or of metal. The lightest satisfactory fenders available are the plastic models made by Bluemels (now part of a company called SKS) and those made by ESGE, while very elegant, but mortally expensive ones are available from a number of French suppliers.

To really keep the water that is splashed up from the road at the front wheel from your feet, you will need a mud flap installed at the bottom of the front fender. Very few models available in the US have one of these things attached, but you can make your own, using a 15—20 cm (6—8 in) square piece of flexible, but relatively firm plastic sheet.

## Lights

Next to fenders, bicycle lights are perhaps the most maligned accessories in the US. In many other countries they are obligatory — for good reasons, as you will appreciate If you have ever experienced how an unlit cyclist appears out of nowhere in your car or bike headlights during darkness or at dusk. The fact that you didn't run into the turkey does not prove that it is safe to go without lights: the risk is infinitely greater without than it is with lights.

Many cyclists argue they never ride in the dark anyway. However, from experience I can report that just about every one who told me that was not only lying, but also playing with his or her life. Sooner or later, you will run into a situation where you are not able to return home before dark. In short, though you may not plan on using lights, you should have them available in case you do need them.

Bicycle lights may be either battery-operated or powered by means of a generator. The latter models are almost invariably installed permanently, while most battery models may be simply removed from the bike. The removability may be good or bad: bad if it's stolen when you do leave it on, good if you can avoid somebody messing around with it by taking it off yourself. Even if the lights are not stolen or vandalized, they may get damaged, so it will be wise to check their operation regularly and to tighten all mechanical and electric connections.

It is possible to use an easily removable form of dynamo lighting. In that case, you will have to make do without a rear light, which is perhaps justified if you use a really big reflector in the rear, making sure it is never obstructed. Removable units are installed to the front fork and consist of a dynamo with light attached (Fig. 5.5). The most satisfactory bicycle generator desing is that of the Swiss Nordlicht with narrow rubber roller. This roller is best adjusted to run off the rim (rather than the tire side wall like all other models). Just keep the rim clean to ensure adequate friction.

The many possible trouble sources of most generator lighting systems, and the physical resistance caused by their mechanical inefficiency, are the reasons why many cyclists prefer battery lights. The batteries and the bulbs must match the light unit: some use a single flat (and hard-to-get) European 4.5 volt battery, other models two D-cells, still others two C-cells. In general, the larger the battery, the more powerful and longer lasting the light is likely to be.

Special lights, powered by a large rechargeable battery, are also available. Since the bicycle commuter's routine tends to be a regular and predicatable one, rechargeable lignts are not a bad idea in his case: it is simple enough to recharge the batteries in a daily routine.

Rechargeable NiCad (nickel-cadmium) batteries stay equally bright until their charge is depleted, and then go out quite suddenly. So make sure the battery is charged regularly, or that you have charged spares with you, since there is no warning when the light will go off. Normal carbon-zinc batteries produce a gradually decreasing electric output over the battery's life. Replace such batteries when the light begins to dim — don't wait until the thing is virtually dead.

If you have to leave the bike out in the rain, you'd better remove the battery lights, or at least their batteries, and store them in a dry place. This stops them from swelling up, becoming useless themselves and damaging the light unit to boot.

Make sure to get correctly rated bulbs for the batteries used, both in terms of voltage and wattage or amperage. I suggest using krypton or halogen gas filled bulbs. The latter are brighter when new, while both types stay equally bright

throughout their useful lifespan, whereas regular bulbs dim to less than half their original ight output.

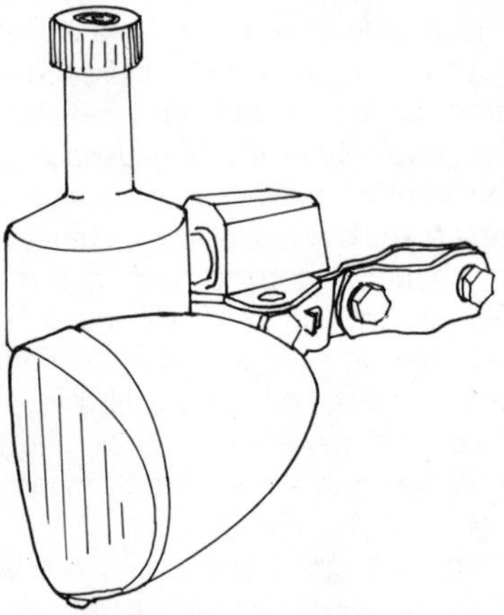

## Reflectors

In addition to lights, some reflectors are quite useful. But they can not completely replace lights, and some reflectors are of no protective benefit whatsoever. The CPSC requirement that all bicycles sold in the US must be equipped with a whole plethora of reflectors is a big step in the wrong direction. Sadly, this was promptly followed by equally inept agencies in other countries.

The fully reflectorized bike gives people the false conviction to be adequately protected with the wrong equipment. Add to that the particular models prescribed show up brightly only under certain obvious but irrelevant conditions, and you've been fooled. Useful is only a big rear reflector (and perhaps pedal reflectors in addition), even as a substitute for a rear light. It must be mounted where it can not be obstructed.

Fig. 5.5 Block generator

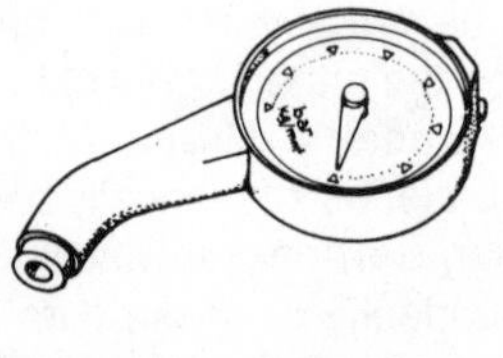

Fig. 5.6 Tire pressure gauge

## Pump and Tire Gauge

You will need to keep your tires inflated properly. Don't count on having gas stations handily available to inflate your tires, and don't just guess at the pressure. For efficient and trouble-free cycling, an adequate tire pressure is important, both to minimize rolling resistance and to protect the tire against damage. If you are experienced enough to have developed a calibrated thumb, you may do without a tire pressure gauge, shown in Fig. 5.6, to check the pressure, but nobody should go without a pump.

The pump should be a model suitable for developing an adequately high pressure. Depending on tire size and design, that may be anywhere from 3—7 bar (45—105 psi) gauge pressure. Be guided by the pressure quoted on the tire sidewalls as an absolute minimum and don't hesitate to inflate especially the one in the rear up to 1 bar (15 psi) more for use on normal roads.

Make sure both the pump and the gauge have a connection that corresponds to the type of valve used. Don't use a hand pump with a flexible hose connector, since the air trapped in the hose makes it impossible to reach an adequate pressure. For quick tire inflation at home, you may keep a big stand pump, which has enough volume to work fine with a flexible hose connector.

Nowadays, pumps are mostly designed to clamp directly between the bike's top tube and bottom bracket along the seat tube. These are referred to as frame-fit pumps and are available in several sizes to match a range of frame sizes each. Many bikes have a peg along the bottom of the top tube — on these, the pump fits between it and the seat lug.

If the pump does not work properly, tighten the screwed nozzle and if necessary replace the underlying rubber washer that seals around the valve.

Take care to install it the right way round, so it doesn't leak even more afterwards.

### Water Bottle and Cage

Though not needed if you work a twenty minutes' ride away from home, the water bottle may be a useful accessory. This applies especially in hot weather and for longer rides — not only to drink, but also for a quick clean-up (also carry a small towel and a comb in your bag). Fig. 5.7 shows both a bottle and the cage in which it is installed on the bike. In case your bike lacks the bosses, most bottle cages are sold complete with a pair of rather crude clips to put around a frame tube. If you need to mount the thing that way, first stick a tire patch around the frame tube, as explained before.

There are lots of other uses for the bottle and its cage. Some health food types of my aquaintance store anything from sun flower seeds to vitamin pills in the bottle. In fact, the bottle is as useful to keep things dry (like the batteries of your lights) as it is to hold liquids. The

In urban cycling, you will often have to leave your bike unattended. This is the type of lock to use and the way to lock it: all parts of the bike locked up together and to something firmly embedded.

cage can be used to hold a tool pouch or any other small bag.

## The Lock

Unfortunately, a good lock is an essential commuting accessory, especially if you are not fortunate enough to work at a place that makes protected bike parking available. My first commuting bike in the US was stolen in front of my downtown office building with the company security guards looking on passively. The very best lock is barely good enough to hold on to your bike in many parts of the world nowadays. The most reliable locks are the large U-locks, such as the ones made by Kryptonite and Citadel. They may be installed by means of a special bracket, which is best at-

tached to the top tube, with the lock hanging down.

Don't just lock the bike onto itself, but secure it to some immovable object. Though the U-locks fit nicely around many street furnishings, you may also want to use a strong cable or chain with end loops or shackles big enough to fit the lock. This allows you to tie the bike up to something bigger, and also lock the various bits and pieces of the bike up to each other. Make sure to select an object from which the lock can not be lifted off: a chain around a parking meter is of little use if the cable can be slipped over the top.

Even with the best lock, you may not be able to completely protect your bike, equipment and accessories against

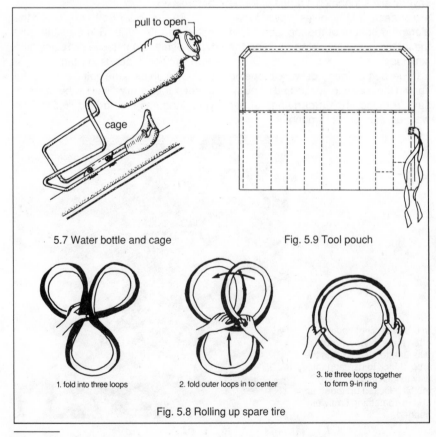

5.7 Water bottle and cage

pull to open

cage

Fig. 5.9 Tool pouch

1. fold into three loops

2. fold outer loops in to center

3. tie three loops together to form 9-in ring

Fig. 5.8 Rolling up spare tire

vandalism and theft of individual items. The smartest thing to do is to be totally paranoid and suspect thieves and thugs everywhere and anytime. Never go anywhere without securing your gear. If at all possible, don't leave your equipment out of sight. When out shopping or taking care of other business, take everything you can't lock up with you in a bag that you carry on your body.

### Warning Devices

When travelling in congested downtown areas or on off-road facilities with joggers and dog-walkers, you may have to alert others to your presence for your (and their) own protection. I have tried using a bell, which is required in many countries, but never noticed any useful reaction amongst other path users — 'It's only a cyclist,' they seem to think when they hear its timid sound. Even shouting something mildly threatening is generally more effective. Alternately, you can use a compressed gas powered sound horn that can be carried in your back pocket.

### Tools and Spares

Depending on a number of factors, you should carry some tools and spare parts on longer rides. How many you need depends on several factors, including the distance. I like to be well prepared, so I can at least get to work in reasonable time, even if something does go wrong — if only to uphold the bike commuters' reputation of responsibility and respectability. Here's a list of the essentials that should probably always be taken along:

*    A set of three tire irons;

*    A tire patch kit, containing patches, rubber solution, chalk, sand paper, talcum powder and a piece of canvas to mend a damaged tire casing.;

*    A small screw driver with a 4 mm ($^3$/16 in) wide blade;

Kuwahara 'city bikes' as sold in the European market, where bicycling for utilitarian purposes is more common than in the US. Though sold 'naked'in the US, there they are equipped with accessories to make them perfect for commuting: fenders, racks and lights.

\*    Crescent wrench (adjustable spanner), 6 or 8 inches long;

\*    Allan keys in whatever sizes correspond to the recessed hexagon bolts used on your bike;

\*    Crank extractor tool, especially the wrench part, which will be needed to tighten a loose crank;

\*    Waterless hand cleaning paste;

\*    Cleaning rags to wipe your hands, as well as protect or clean any messy parts before working on them.

Additionally, you may want to take the following special tools if your commute is a long one:

\*    Spoke wrench to straighten a bent wheel;

\*    Chain rivet tool to take the chain apart and join it up again;

\*    A pair of small pliers, such as needle nose pliers, with sharp cutters;

\*    Spare parts: spokes of correct length, brake cable, tube, chain links and lighting parts. If you also take a spare tire, turn it into three loops, as shown in Fig. 5.8.

When buying tools, get the best.That means expensive ones, exactly fitting the parts in question. Don't let terms like 'economy tools' fool you: in the long run the best tools are much more economic than any cheap tool will ever be, since the former lasts forever, while the latter quickly wears out and may actually damage the bike's components.

## Tool Pouch

I suggest you carry the tools and spares in a pouch that holds all the tools you ever plan to carry and has a few spare slots. If you can't buy one ready-made, it will be easy enough to sew your own. Be guided by Fig. 5.9, using a strong material such as denim from an old pair of blue jeans. Allow enough space between the various items to enable you to roll it all together when it is full.

Of course, having all the tools in the world does not necessarily solve any problems. So you should learn to handle them and carry out basic repairs on the bike. At a minimum, you should learn to handle the adjustments and repairs that are explained in various places in this book. It will be even better to buy a special repair manual, such as my *Bicycle Repair Book* and get so familiar with your bike that you can handle virtually all repairs yourself.

## Bicycle Computer

Hardly essential for commuting, but it is interesting to record your progress. Meant is an electronic speedometer. Generally consisting of a readout unit to be mounted on the handlebars and a sensor that picks up the impulses from a magnet installed on the front wheel, this is your basic guide to riding speed and mileage. Get one with as few buttons as possible and remove it from the bike whenever you have to leave it unguarded.

# 6. Dress Right for Commuting

Bicycle commuting, like any other kind of cycling, is more comfortable if you dress for the work at hand. Even so, at times it will be more practical to wear the kind of gear you are expected to wear in business, even to ride your bike. If the distance is modest — say up to about three miles one way — there will be no need to change into special cycling clothing.

Just the same, for most people who have to ride more than just a few miles, cycling clothing can be helpful, certainly if you can also count on a place to change and wash up at the other end. In the present chapter, not only the cute, fashionable, colorful, tight-fitting bicycle clothing will be described, but also the kind of gear to wear when the weather is less than perfect.

### Cycling Dress

First we shall look at normal cycling wear. Bicycle clothing is probably the most functional gear ever designed for any sport, and though there'll be no need to ride around looking to all the world like a bicycle racer in full competition, it makes sense to aim at the same comfort that has been achieved to accommodate racers. Besides, in recent years bicycle clothing — and fitness clothing in general — has become high fashion in some circles. It has been developed thanks to the use of modern fabrics and bright colors to look good, rather than weird, as it did only a decade ago.

This gear has been designed the way it is to provide the freedom of movement, the control of temperature and humidity and the protection against chafing that allows a racer to continue non- stop for seven hours, covering 150 miles or more. That, I'm sure, will also be comfortable when riding to work and back.

I shall highlight the points that make the various items of bicycle clothing so suitable for their purpose. These will also be the things to watch out for when buying clothing that is not specifically designed for the purpose, to determine whether it will serve you anyway. You may refer to Fig. 6.1 for an idea of what a typical racing outfit looks like.

### Shoes and Socks

The shoes are perhaps the single most important item that can make the difference between effective cycling and plodding along. Special bicycling shoes consist of light leather uppers with a thin

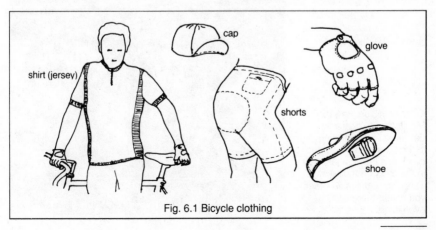

shirt (jersey) — cap — glove — shorts — shoe

Fig. 6.1 Bicycle clothing

but very stiff sole, generally with a metal plate built in to achieve that stiffness. This helps distribute the pedaling force over a large area of the foot. Consequently, the pressure at any one point of the foot is within the comfortable range, and a more efficient transfer of power from the legs to the bicycle drivetrain results.

Bicycling shoes either have metal or plastic cleats or a patent 'clipless' clamping device similar to a miniature ski binding, to hold the feet in place on the pedals. There is little doubt that either system allows more secure pedaling, especially on long trips where there is rarely a need to get off the bike. However, these things make it nearly impossible to walk, and tricky enough to get on and off.

As a bicycle commuter, you will probably want to be able to walk in reasonable comfort as well. That not only rules out most clipless binding systems, but also makes old fashioned cleats highly inconvenient. Either you do without cleats or you should have a

spare pair of shoes easily accessible for getting around when off the bike.

In addition to the real things, compromise solutions in the form of walking/cycling shoes exist these days. They have stiff, slightly profiled plastic soles and well ventilated uppers. The cloth uppers unfortunately cause your feet to get saturated almost instantaneously in the rain — more about that under *Rain Gear* below. Similarly, cycling in cold weather poses special problems, which will also be covered separately.

Whatever kind of shoes you wear, they must have the right length and width not to hurt. Pull the shoe laces relatively tight in the upper part of the closure, so that the toes do not slip forward, getting pushed against the front of the shoe. Inside the shoes, choose cotton or wool socks that absorb perspiration. To be comfortable, they should be relatively thick, especially in the sole, and they should not have a knotty seam in the toe area. If you wear street clothes, get socks that are long and elastic enough to fit over your pant legs to keep the latter out of the chain.

Off to work, on his $1500 Moulton bike, specially delivered to the starting site in the trunk of the car, and carrying a full business suit in the bags on the bike. This kind of dress will keep you comfortable cycling, even in quite cool weather.

## Shorts and Pants

Specific bicycle shorts are tight but stretchable knitted garments with rather long tight-fitting legs and a high waist. They generally stretch so elastically that they stay up without the need for a belt, though suspenders may be required, depending on your body build. Sewn in the crotch area is a soft and smooth piece of chamois leather, which protects the skin against chafing and absorbs perspiration. Correctly worn directly over the bare skin, they must be washed out daily. Consequently, you need at least two pairs to make sure you always have a clean pair.

Old fashioned woollen pants have the advantage that they regulate your body temperature better and get less smelly when they absorb perspiration. On the other hand, synthetics take up less moisture, dry a lot faster, and are much easier to wash.

One other way of minimizing the laundry problem is by wearing very light, stretchy seamless underpants underneath the cycling shorts. These items are available as regular women's underwear or may be obtained in men's versions from some bicycle outfits. The latest item in this line is women's panties with a piece of (simulated) chamois sewn in, intended to be worn underneath a dress, but also suitable to be worn under any other kind of civil wear, presumably for men and women alike.

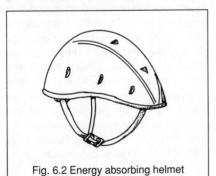

Fig. 6.2 Energy absorbing helmet

In addition to ordinary bicycle shorts and long legged cold weather versions of these same things, there are special bicycle touring shorts and slacks that are quite practical.

Whatever kind of pants you wear, they can only be comfortable if they are smooth and soft. Stretchable materials are best and they should have no bulky seams. Slacks must be tight enough around the lower leg not to get caught in the chain. If they are not quite tight enough there, tuck the legs inside your socks or keep them together by means of elastic straps with a Velcro closure.

## Shirts and Tops

The bicycling shirt, or jersey, is a tight fitting knitted garment with short sleeves, a very long bodice and pockets sewn on in the back. It works well to absorb perspiration, covers the parts of the torso that should be protected even when bending over, and doesn't flap in the wind. Similar things with long sleeves are designed for colder weather. Both long and short sleeved cycling shirts are available in wool and various synthetics. The former material is really most comfortable in colder weather.

When it gets cooler, you may either wear a regular long sleeved cycling jersey or a thin, tightly fitting sweater over the top. Except in freezing weather, get a model that can be opened at the neck by means of a zipper. You may also wear a light windproof jacket over the top of your shirt, providing it is made of a densely woven material that allows air and perspiration through.

## Gloves

Even in warm weather, special cycling gloves are highly recommended, since they make the ride a lot more comfortable. This applies especially to riders who select a low riding style, which places a rather high percentage of their weight on the hands. These gloves have leather insides and open knit top panels and have fingers cut off to a length of about an inch (2.5 cm). The palm area should be padded. If you do not like to wear gloves, at least use foam handlebar sleeves instead of (or underneath) regular handlebar tape, since this also provides the kind of cushioning effect needed to prevent nerve damage in the area of the palms. For colder weather, special winter cycling gloves are available, as described below.

### Head Protection

Back in the sixties and early seventies, head protection might at best have meant something to keep the rain off your head. Today, at least American and Canadian cyclists have ample choice of real accident protection for their heads (see Fig. 6.2). In other countries the hard shell helmet, as it is generally called, is taking a long time to get established.

I suggest you wear one, though I'll be the last person in the world to propose making helmets mandatory: you're the person to decide what to do with your head. Meanwhile, refer to Chapters 10 and 11 for more details on the safety aspect of head protection.

Today's bike helmets available in the US all satisfy the elementary safety criteria. The most comfortable ones are the lightest. Fashion has played a role here too, with the unlined styrofoam models with separate fabric cover leading the way. These things are comfortable to wear, well ventilated, and attached in such a way that they do not move out of place upon impact. Most of these important criteria are satisfied if the helmet meets the American standard ANSI Z-90.4. Many helmets can be combined with a shield or visor to keep the sun out of your eyes, or the rain off your glasses.

There is one situation where a helmet becomes too uncomfortable to wear for most people. That happens on a steep climb in hot weather. This situation is characterized by a combination of profuse perspiration, due to the heat generated as the result of performing work close to your maximum output, with the low speed that virtually precludes natural ventilation induced by air movement. I simply take off the helmet in a case like that. Just don't forget to put it back on as soon as the descent begins.

### Civil Clothes

Perhaps it is ridiculous to overemphasize the use of bicycle clothing, as I have done in the preceding sections. Of course, you can ride in normal street clothes, and if you have to do other things on the way, so you should.

Even in regular commuting it often makes sense to dress like a normal business person. Considering the time it takes to get changed and the hassle involved, you may well decide to wear a normal set of clothes, leaving perhaps only a tie and a jacket (or whatever achieves the same effect for a working woman) at work to slip on after you get there. When dressed like this — certainly in hot weather — you may have to temper your desire to cycle fast, so you don't perspire like a pig most of the day.

What does make sense, certainly when your trip is more than marginal in length, is to select civil looking clothes with cycling in mind. Not all pants are equally suitable: avoid wide legs and materials that loose their shape and their crease. Wear socks that are long and elastic enough to hold the pant legs down. Wear shoes that are light and firm enough to provide cycling comfort — and don't scuff too easily. Similarly, a lilly white shirt or blouse is probably not as suitable as a discretely patterned version.

### Rain Gear

Yes, it is entirely possible to ride a bike in the rain, even if it is to get to work and back. In my native Holland you'd never get very far if you'd stop for every shower. Yet more people commute by bike there than anywhere else in the western world. Besides equipping the bike to keep the rain and spray off your body and the bike, you can make sure to have clothing that will see you through a heavy shower in reasonable comfort.

For the short ride, there is an easy solution, acceptable as long as the temperature is above about 60 degrees F (18 degrees C): get wet. Once you get to the office or home, you can wipe yourself and put dry clothes on, assuming you keep a set of clothes at work and have adequate facilities for changing. However, if you don't want to bother changing clothes — especially for longer commutes — and for lower temperatures, you will need special rain gear.

Both this kind of clothing and the material described for cold weather cycling in the next section justify the perusal of a couple of bicycle mail order catalogs. Most of these companies have a summer and a winter catalog, the latter one often containing lots of useful items in this field, complete with worthwhile information on the properties of various materials and designs.

Fig. 6.3 illustrates some typical rain garments. The big problem is that perfectly waterproof materials don't only keep rain out, but also perspiration in. Even if you are not usually aware of it, the cyclist is continuously perspiring as a result of performing the work necessary to propel his machine. Normally, this perspiration evaporates immediately as it is absorbed by the air passing along the body. When an impermeable barrier in the form of a waterproof coated fabric prevents this natural process, the moisture condenses on the inside of the barrier and very soon it penetrates every

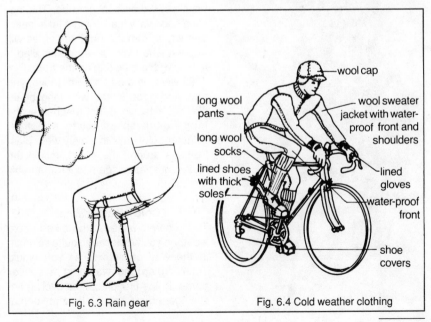

Fig. 6.3 Rain gear                                        Fig. 6.4 Cold weather clothing

long wool pants

long wool socks

lined shoes with thick soles

wool cap

wool sweater jacket with waterproof front and shoulders

lined gloves

water-proof front

shoe covers

fiber between your body and the rain gear, until you are as dismally soaked as you would have been without rain wear.

The only satisfactory solution to this dilemma is the use of a special material that is just porous enough to pass water vapor, without allowing the passage of liquid water. One material that satisfies this criterion is Goretex, a trade name for a cloth consisting of woven fabric with a barrier layer of stretched PTFE. There are a few other materials and coatings that do the same after a fashion.

Though most garments made with these materials are awfully expensive and often garishly styled, I consider the investment absolutely essential in most

Not your typical American cycling wear. But it is interesting to note that the Dutch have no inhibition about wearing such fashionable rain gear, even for cycling. Of course, they also have the bikes to match

climates at any time, and at least for off-season cycling in more blessed regions. Available are jackets, capes, coats, pants and suits, designed either specifically for cycling or for general use. Try a number of different models out in a cycling or backpacking store, to make sure you get items that are not so generously cut as to hinder you while cycling.

Personally, I find the rain cape is still the best solution, provided it is combined with spats. The latter are a kind of leggings that are open in the back. They may be either home-made or purchased from the only known source of these things in the US, Custom Cycling Fitments. The cape should preferably be a model without a built-in hood. A hood would restrict your peripheral vision, which is especially important when checking behind before turning off. The best thing to keep your head dry is a helmet without vent holes — or a model with a rainproof cover.

Finally, with regard to rain gear, the feet are a real problem. Cycling shoes are little use when it comes to keeping your feet dry on a longer ride. This applies especially if a constant jet is being thrown up from the front wheel, as will happen when you have not installed a fender with a mud flap on the front.

To ward off the rain from above, you may find good spats, with long beak-shaped extensions that reach over the tops of the shoes, quite effective. Another solution is to simply wear plastic bags around the socks, inside the shoes: not very elegant, but remarkably effective.

### Cold Weather Wear

To be comfortable on the bike in cold weather, you will not need quite so much in the way of clothing as you would standing around watching a soccer game. In the first place, the cycling activity generates enough heat to keep at least your trunk reasonably warm. In the second place, all that gear would hinder your movements. The heat is mainly generated in the trunk and the upper legs, so these parts will keep warm more easily, while the extremities of ears, hands and feet may need much thicker clothing.

Since the relatively high speed at which the cyclist proceeds causes high resultant air velocities, excessive wind chill may ensue in many cases. That is especially critical during descents, when the speed is high and your output low. Consequently, bicycling will cause additional problems, since you will be experiencing all the extremes. You'll be doing hard heat-producing work without significant wind cooling when climbing, and cold fast air-cooled descents.

To arm yourself for that, dress in layers that are easily put on and taken off. In addition, the wind must be kept out, for which a wind-proof outer layer is needed. That means a rather closely fitting long jacket, made of very densely woven cloth that is permeable to water vapor, preferably in two-layer construction. This same kind of outer shell protects you best when a cold wind would cut right through the warmest woollen wear.

Underneath this outer layer, wear several relatively thin layers of other warm materials. Close fitting knitted or other very stretchable materials are ideal. For long underwear, polypropylene is a good solution, since it is very light and not as hard on the skin as many other synthetics and wool. As for design, all these garments must be long, close fitting and easy to put on or take off. Zippers and other closures should be installed in such a way that there is a large enough overlap to keep the cold out, especially in the front.

Hands and feet cause greater problems, since the body's thermostat turns off the supply of heat-carrying blood to these extremities whenever the temperature of head and trunk is in danger of falling below the vital organs' required minimum operating temperature. Thick woollen socks inside special thick-soled and lined winter cycling shoes keep the feet comfortable. Add plastic bags, as described above for rain wear, if the combination of cold with rain or sleet occurs. Alternately, you may find pedal covers keep the feet comfortable

Wear what is comfortable on the bike. You can change into more businesslike attire once you get to your destination. Los Angeles photographer Ben Swets does it all the time. He often has to do this transformation before reaching the site of his business engagement. Most commuters can do it more conveniently at work.

under such conditions. Nylon backed woollen gloves or relatively light lined leather models, such as cross-country skiing gloves, may suffice for the hands. Thick lined mittens may be needed when it gets even colder.

For the head, finally, a helmet without air scoops will be most comfortable, or a rainproof helmet cover for a model with. In very cold climates, you may want to wear a thin cap underneath the helmet to cover the ears and other exposed portions of your head. And if you elect not to wear a helmet, you can get a knitted wool cap, as shown in Fig. 6.4.

Though hard to find in the US, there are specific winter riding garments of the kind that is readily available in traditional cycling countries like France and England. If you should ever get there on your travels, don't forget to stock up on such useful things while you get the chance. These garments are integrated items that combine the warm materials in a design specifically intended for cycling, with wind breaking panels in the front of jacket and pants. Fig. 6.4 shows a cyclist wearing such gear. In addition, there are special add-ons to normal cycling garments that can be put on or taken off easily, although they look awful. These are particularly convenient at times and in areas where significant temperature differences are encountered, such as in hilly and windy coastal regions.

# Part II – Handling the Bike

# 7. Basic Set-up and Riding

The chapters of this second part of the book are primarily devoted to the skills and knowledge that are prerequisite to the safe and enjoyable practice of bicycle commuting. Some of this material may also be found in general bicycle books. However, only here is the practical background of cycling for transportation specifically considered.

This particular chapter will first help you arrive at the adjustments that are necessary to cycle in comfort. This is followed by practical advice on posture, riding style and the methods that allow you to cycle continuously at speed. Excluded from this material will be the subject of gearing choice and pedaling rate, since these topics are covered comprehensively in Chapter 8.

### Riding Posture

To cycle fast with endurance, the conventional idea of a comfortable position must be reconsidered. Though bicycle racers have long known that they are most comfortable in a relatively low crouched position, most other cyclists — whatever kind of bike they ride — seem to feel that to be comfortable one has to sit upright. That may be fine for folks who travel only short distances at low speed in easy terrain. However, the serious commuting bicyclist has much more in common with the racer than he has with these occasional short distance cyclists.

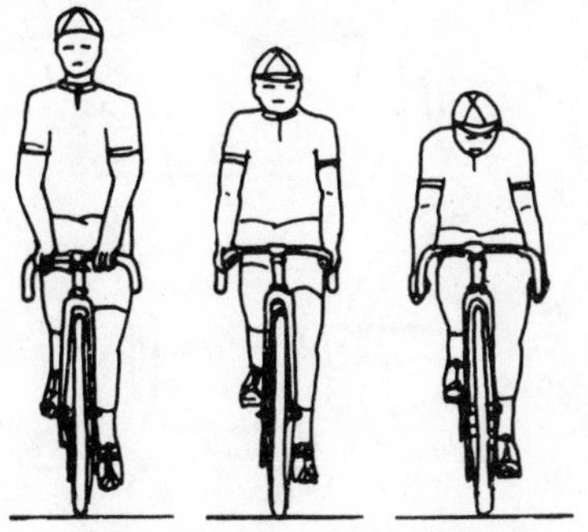

Fig. 7.1 shows the three basic kinds of riding posture for comparison: upright, inclined and fully crouched. The cyclist who rides in the upright position may well be convinced this is the only comfortable way to ride a bike. As I look out of my window, I see at least thirty people cycling by in this posture each hour. Those who are going north have a very slight uphill — only a 1% slope. All are working hard; you can tell by the strained expression on their faces, their cramped movements and their abysmally slow progress. Every now and again another type of cyclist comes by. Passing the others at twice their speed and obviously more relaxed, these are the ones who ride in either a deep incline or in a fully crouched position.

There are of course also other reasons why the latter are going faster and suffering less, but the first and most important step towards this more comfortable style is their different riding posture. In the lower position, the rider's weight is divided more evenly over handlebars, saddle and pedals. Firstly, this reduces the pressure on the rider's buttocks. Secondly, it allows the relaxed fast pedaling technique so essential for long duration power output. Thirdly, it enables restraining the upper body to bring more force to bear on the pedals. Finally, it can reduce the wind resistance.

Fig. 7.1 Three riding postures

Wind resistance is a major factor in cycling, especially when traveling fast or against the wind. The cyclist's frontal area is crucial to the wind resistance, and is much lower in the more inclined positions, which is reflected in the power required to ride the bike at the same speed.

Strangely enough, many people to whom the advantages have been demonstrated nevertheless insist on riding in the upright position. They bring all sorts of arguments, ranging from, "That's only for racing" to, "That is terribly uncomfortable" or, "You couldn't cycle any distance that way." The undeniable fact is that they are fooling themselves. In reality, they are less comfortable, whatever they think, and have to do more work to proceed at the same speed or to cover the same distance. Get accustomed to the right posture early in your cycling career, and you'll be a more effective cyclist, one who gets less frustration and more pleasure out of the pursuit.

### The Basic Posture

Even within the general range of comfortable positions, there are enough different variants to allow changes and adaptations. This makes it possible to adapt to different conditions and gives you the chance to vary your position from time to time. The latter helps avoid the numbing feeling when pressure is applied in the same location for a longer period. Especially the position of the hands may require some variation, certainly if the cyclist is not yet used to supporting a significant portion of his own weight on the arms.

The following sections will describe just how the saddle and the handlebars should be set to achieve the basic relaxed position that is shown in Fig. 7.2. This particular posture is worth looking into a little closer. Study the proportions, noting also that merely holding the handlebars in a different location allows adequate variation. This may be required to apply more force to the pedals or to reduce the wind resistance by lowering the front, or to get a better overview of the road or the scenery by raising the front by as little as perhaps 10 cm (4 in) either way. The following description is based on the assumption that you have a drop handlebar derailleur bicycle of the right size to match your physique.

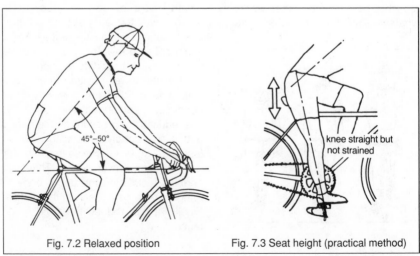

45°–50°

knee straight but not strained

Fig. 7.2 Relaxed position                    Fig. 7.3 Seat height (practical method)

## Saddle Height

The height of the saddle, or rather the distance of its top relative to the pedals, is the most critical variable for effective cycling. It should be adjusted so that the leg can be stretched comfortably without straining the knee, which would cause excessive force and rotation of the joint. At the same time, the distance between the pedal in its highest point and the saddle must be such that the knee is not bent excessively.

Here I shall describe three methods of establishing the correct seat height. These are all good enough for preliminary set-up and the first thousand miles of cycling. Your ultimate seat position may require additional individual experimental fine-tuning, based on your subjective long-term comfort. On the other hand, in the vast majority of all cases, each of these techniques will lead to a satisfactory seat position, without the need for subsequent fine-tuning.

The first method is illustrated in Fig. 7.3. You should wear cycling shoes with flat heels. Place the bike next to a wall or post for support when you sit on it. Adjust the seat up or down (following the adjustment procedure below) until it is set at such a height relative to the pedal that the heel of your cycling shoe rests on the pedal when your knee is straight but not strained, with the pedal down, crank in line with the seat tube.

Sit on the bike and place the heels on the pedals. Symmetrical pedals can be merely turned upside down; on platform models the toeclips must be removed. Pedal backwards this way, making sure you do not have to rock from side to side to reach the pedals. Now raise the saddle 12 mm ($^1/2$ in) above this height. Tighten the saddle in this position. Note that this heels-on-pedals style only applies to determining the seat height, not to riding the bike, as described below.

The second method is referred to as 109% rule. It was developed at Loughborough University in England and is illustrated in Fig. 7.4. To use this method, first measure your inseam leg length by standing with your back against a wall with the legs straight, the feet about 10cm (4 in) apart, wearing thin soled shoes with flat heels. Make a pencil mark for the location of the crotch on the wall. This is easiest to do with the aid of a drawing triangle or a rectangular board held upright and pushed up against the wall between the legs. Measure the vertical distance between this mark and the floor.

Now multiply the figure so found by 1.09. That is presumed to be the optimal distance between the top of the saddle and the pedal axle when the pedal is down, crank in line with the seat tube. Measure it out and set the seat accordingly with the plane connecting front and back of the saddle top horizontal. How

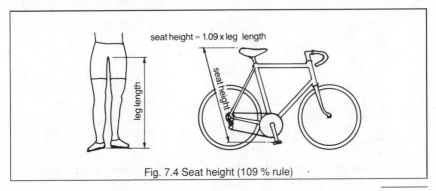

Fig. 7.4 Seat height (109 % rule)

the saddle is raised or lowered will be explained below.

The third method, illustrated in Fig. 7.5, was developed by the American bicycle racing coach Mark Hodges. It is probably the most accurate method. You will need a helper to measure and a calculator to figure out the correct saddle height. Stand barefoot upright with your back against a wall, the feet 15 cm (6 in) apart. Now measure the distance from the floor over the ankle joint and the knee joint to the greater trochanter. That's the outwardmost bump on the femur, or hip, which coincides with the hip joint's center of rotation: when you raise the leg this point does not move.

To establish the optimal seat height, measured between the top of the saddle near its center and the center of the pedal axle (crank pointing down in line with the seat tube), multiply the dimension so found by 0.96. If appropriate, add an allowance for thick soles, thick cleats or special clipless pedals with matching shoes.

Even after using any of these methods, you may have to do some fine-tuning to achieve long-term comfort. Riders with disproportionately small feet may want to place the saddle a little lower, those with big feet perhaps slightly higher. No need to get carried away: raise or lower the seat in steps of about 5 mm ($^1$/4 in) at a time and try to get used to any position by riding several hundred miles, or several weeks, before attempting any change, which must again be in the order of about 5 mm to make any real difference.

When cycling, the ball of the foot (the second joint of the big toe) should be over the center of the pedal axle, or spindle, with the heel raised so much that the knee is never straightened fully. Not all cyclists incline the foot equally; consequently, the amount by which the saddle is moved relative to the point determined may vary a little for different riders — a matter of 5 mm ($^1$/4 in) one way or the other.

### Saddle Position and Angle

The normal preliminary saddle position is such that the seat post is roughly in the middle of the saddle. For optimal pedaling efficiency, adjust the saddle forward or backwards after it has been set to the correct height, as explained in the preceding section. On any bike designed on conventional lines, sitting on the bike with the foot under the toeclip and the crank placed horizontally, the center of the knee joint must be vertical-

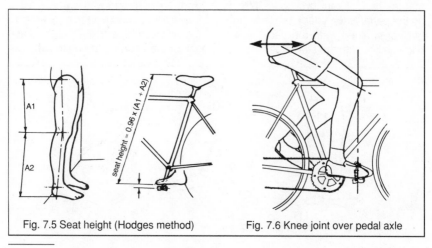

Fig. 7.5 Seat height (Hodges method)        Fig. 7.6 Knee joint over pedal axle

ly aligned with the spindle of the forward pedal, as shown in Fig. 7.6.

The angle of the saddle relative to the horizontal plane should initially be set so as to keep the line that connects the highest points at the front and the back level. After the handlebars have been set to the correct height, it may be necessary to modify this angle to prevent slipping forward or backwards. This too may not become apparent until after some miles of cycling. Adjusting procedures for both forward position and angle are outlined below.

### Saddle Adjustments

To do the actual mechanical adjusting work on the saddle, first take a close look at the way it is installed on the bike,

One bike that has to be set up each time to ride it: the Bickerton folding bike. It is light and easy to carry, as well as to set up. A good choice for those who have to commute partway on public transportation or combine biking with car pooling.

comparing it with Fig. 3.11 in Chapter 3. The saddle height is adjusted by loosening the binder bolt behind the seat lug, raising or lowering the saddle with the attached seat post in a twisting motion, and then tightening the binder bolt again at the required height, making sure it is straight. On mountain bikes and hybrids, this process is simplified by the quick-release binder bolt.

To change the forward position, undo the adjustment bolts (only one bolt on some models) on your adjustable seat post. These bolts are usually reached from under the saddle cover, though they can be reached from below or the side on some models. Once loosened, push the saddle forward or backwards until the desired position is reached; then tighten the bolts, making sure the saddle is held under the desired angle relative to the horizontal plane.

### Handlebar Height and Position

The highest point of the handlebars should always be lower than the top of the saddle to ride efficiently. Just how much lower will be determined by the shape of the handlebars and the rider's physiognomy. It depends on the relative distribution of body weight and torso height, as well as on the upper and lower arm length. That's why only experiments can tell what will eventually be right for any particular rider. Here I shall merely tell you how to determine the position for an initial relaxed posture. After about a thousand miles of cycling, you should be able to fine-tune the handlebar height and stem length to match your needs perfectly.

The following description is again based on the use of a correctly dimensioned frame, as outlined in Chapter 3. In order to make sure it is not too high, first check whether the fully crouched position can be achieved. Place the handlebars in their lowest possible position and, sitting on the saddle, hold them in the lowest part of the bend (below the brake levers). With the lower arms horizontal and the elbows under a slightly acute angle, the upper body should now lie almost horizontally. This is the crouched or 'full tuck' position. It may be necessary to choose a longer or shorter handlebar stem for comfort in this position.

To set the handlebars for a relaxed initial posture, without sacrificing the advantages of the full tuck when conditions call for it, proceed as follows: First set the top of the bars about 3 cm ($1^1/4$ in) lower than the saddle. Sit on the bike and reach forward for the part of the bend between the straight top and the brake lever attachments. In this position your shoulders should be about midway between seat and hands, as shown in Fig. 7.2 at the beginning of this chapter. The arms should feel neither stretched nor heavily loaded and they should run parallel.

If they don't satisfy the last criterion, your handlebar bend is too wide or too narrow; if you can not find a relaxed position, you will need a longer or shorter stem. If you should have a particularly long combination of lower arms and torso in relation to your leg length, you may not be comfortable even with a long stem. In that case, a slightly larger frame, which has a longer top tube as well as a longer seat tube, may be in order. Conversely, long legs combined with short arms and torso may require you use a shorter frame to achieve the right top tube length. In extreme cases of either variety, the right top tube length just cannot be achieved with a bike that fits in height., The ultimate solution in this case would be a custom-built frame with the desired dimensions of seat tube and top tube. However, it is probably not quite so critical that you can't make do with a stock frame.

Finally, grab the handlebar bend at the ends, leaning forward on them while seated. The handlebar angle relative to the horizontal plane should be such that the hands don't slip either into the bend or off towards the ends in this position. If you initially have difficulties achieving this position, you may start off with the handlebars somewhat higher. In that case, the ends must also point down slightly. Lower and level them out as you develop the style that allows you to ride with the lower handlebar position after some practice.

### Handlebar Adjustments

To vary the height of the handlebars, straddle the front wheel. Undo the expander bolt, which is usually recessed in the top of the stem (refer to Fig. 3.9 in Chapter 3). If the stem does not come loose immediately, you may have to lift the handlebars to raise the wheel off the ground, then tap on the head of the expander bolt with a hammer. This will loosen the internal clamping device. Now raise or lower the handlebar stem as required. Tighten the expander bolt again, while holding the handlebars straight in the desired position.

To change the angle of the handlebar ends with respect to the horizontal plane, undo the binder bolt that clamps the handlebar bend in the front of the stem. Twist the handlebar bend until it is under the desired angle, and then tighten the binder bolt again, holding the bar centered. To install a longer stem or a different bar design, you are referred to any bicycle maintenance book or your friendly bike store. The correct handlebar position often puts more strain on the hands than beginning cyclists find comfortable, especially when rough road surfaces induce vibrations. Minimize this problem by always keeping the arms slightly bent, never holding them in a cramped position. If you still ex-

perience discomfort, wrap the handlebars with cushioned foam sleeves (such
as Grab-On) instead of normal handlebar tape.

### Adjusting Mountain Bikes

The mountain bike and its younger
sister, the hybrid, are both very suitable
for commuting and should be recommended to those who are new to cycling.
In that case, most of the adjustments
described above also apply as long as
you ride on the road. Since most of your
riding will probably be done on the road,
whatever kind of bike is used, the only
real difference is that the flat mountain
bike handlebars do not allow the lower
position for the full tuck. Consequently,
I suggest you set the saddle and the
handlebars so that the relaxed position
described above is possible when holding the flat bars at the ends.

### Basic Bike Handling

Once saddle and handlebars are adjusted correctly, it will be time to take to
the road on your bike. In case you are
not yet familiar with the derailleur bicycle
and the rest of your equipment, here's
just a suggestion for getting on and off
the bike. More advanced riding and handling techniques involve learning pro-
cesses that will be treated separately in

chapters 8 and 9, but the simple act of
starting and stopping  the bike competently should be mastered immediately.

Before you start off, make sure your
shoe laces are tied and tucked in, or
short enough not to run the risk of getting caught in the chain. Put the bike in
a low gear.

Start off at the side of the road, after
having checked to make sure no traffic
is following closely behind. Straddle the
top tube by swinging the appropriate leg
either over the handlebars, the top tube,
or the saddle. Hold the handlebars with
both hands at the top of the bend. If you
use toeclips, tap against the pedal with
the toe of your starting foot to turn it
around. This brings the toeclip on top,
after which you can slip the foot under
the toeclip. In case you use shoes with
cleats, place the slot of the cleat over the
ridge of the pedal.

Turn the pedal backward until it is in
the top position. Pull the toe strap, but
not quite so tight as to cut off circulation
in the foot, then pedal back three
quarters of a revolution to bring the
pedal to 2 o'clock, just above the
horizontally forward position. Don't tuck
the ends of the toe straps in. If you have
clipless pedals with matching shoes,
learn and practice how the particular

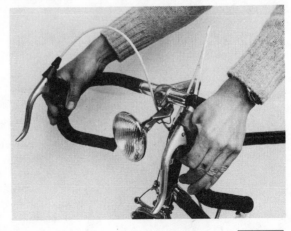

Set the handlebars so that
you can easily reach them
leaning forward in a
moderate incline. A good
position on a bike with
dropped handlebars is with
the hands just over the attachments for the brake
levers. However, on longer
rides, change hand position
from time to time to prevent
fatigue.

model used is inserted and removed first.

Look behind you to make sure the road is clear, then check ahead to establish which course you'll want to follow. Move off by placing your weight on the pedal, leaning lightly on the handlebars. Put the other foot on its pedal as soon as it is in the top position. When you have gained some momentum, tap the toe against the back of the free pedal to turn it over, and right away slide the foot in under the toeclip. Pedal a few more strokes, then pull the loose toestrap taut, securing the second foot to its pedal as well.

To slow down, whether just to stop or to get off the bike, first look behind you again to make sure you are not getting in the way of cyclists or motorists following. Aim for the position where you will want to stop. Change into a lower gear, appropriate for starting off again later. Push against the buckle of the toestrap for whichever foot you want to have free first (or liberate your foot from the clip-

less pedal, if that is what you use), meanwhile pulling the foot up and back to loosen it when that pedal is up. When using cycling shoes with cleats, the strap must be just loose enough to raise the foot to clear the pedal with the cleat.

Slow down by braking gently, using mainly the front brake to stop. When you have come to a standstill, or just before that point, make sure the pedal with the loosened strap is up, then pull the foot up and out. Place it on the ground, leaning over in the same direction, while moving forward off the saddle to straddle the top tube. Now you are in the right position to dismount or start again.

If you want to get off the bike at this point, bring the other foot up, pedaling backwards, and loosen the buckle of the toestrap to release the foot. Now you're ready to get off the bike. However, under most circumstances you will find that the machine is most easily controlled when you remain on the bike, straddling the top tube. Consequently, I suggest you only dismount if it is really necessary.

# 8. Using the Gears

Modern bicycles, in the overwhelming majority, are equipped with a sophisticated derailleur system for multiple gearing. To change gear, the chain is shifted onto any chosen combination of chainring and sprocket with the aid of two derailleur mechanisms.

Nowadays, twelve and fourteen speed systems are generally used, although some have only ten speeds and mountain bikes usually have 18 or 21 speed systems. In the case of ten, twelve or fourteen speed set-ups, two chainrings are used in combination with five, six or seven sprockets, respectively. Fifteen, eighteen and 21-speed systems have three chainrings, combined with five, six or seven sprockets, respectively.

The derailleur method of gearing allows minute adaptations of the gear ratio to the cyclist's potential on the one hand, and the terrain, wind resistance and road conditions on the other hand. All that is mere theory, because in reality the majority of people, including most beginning commuting cyclists, plod along in the wrong gear for the work load. Indeed, learning to select the right gear may well provide the biggest single

step towards improved cycling speed and endurance. That's the subject of the present chapter.

There is a sound theory behind the principle of gear selection, based on the optimal pedaling rate, which I have covered in several of my other books, such as the *Bicycle Racing Guide*. Interesting though this theory is, one need not wait with applying the technique until it is thoroughly understood. That's why I shall outline the correct use of gearing to the extent you will need it at this point.

**The Derailleur System**

Fig. 8.1 shows and names the mechanical components of the derailleur system. The chain runs over two or three chainrings, mounted on the RH crank, and any one of five, six or seven sprockets, mounted on a freewheel block at the rear wheel. As long as you are pedaling forward, the chain can be moved from one chainring to the other with the front derailleur, or changer, and from one sprocket to another by means of the rear derailleur.

Because the various chainrings and sprockets have different numbers of teeth, the ratio between pedaling speed

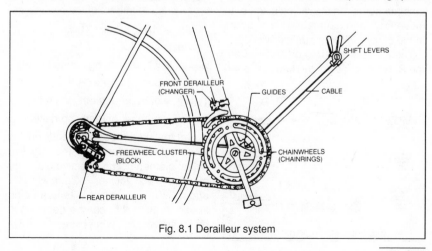

Fig. 8.1 Derailleur system

and the speed with which the rear wheel — and with it the whole bike — is driven changes whenever a different combination is selected. As illustrated in Fig. 8.2, bigger chainrings in the front and smaller sprockets in the rear result in higher gears, smaller chainrings and bigger sprockets give lower gears. Higher gears are selected when cycling is easy, so the available output allows a high riding speed. Select a lower gear when higher resistances must be overcome, such as riding uphill or against a head wind, or when starting off from standstill.

Each derailleur is controlled by means of a shift lever, usually mounted on the frame's down tube. Alternative positions are less convenient on bikes with drop handlebars. Only mountain bikes and most hybrids, with their flat bars, allow the use of thumb shifters, mounted directly on the handlebars, within easy reach from the hand grips. Make sure derailleurs and shifters match and the former are suitable for the kind of terrain you will be encountering. In particular, you need widely spaced gearing if your commute route is very hilly.

Most shifts are made with the rear derailleur, while the front changer is primarily used either to find subtle intermediate gears (on the racing bike), or to move from one general range of gears to the other (on the mountain bike).

The rear derailleur is controlled from the RH shifter. To put the chain on a different sprocket in the rear, move the RH shifter, while pedaling forward with reduced force. Pull the lever back to change to a larger sprocket, which results in a lower gear; push it forward to reach a smaller sprocket, resulting in a higher gear.

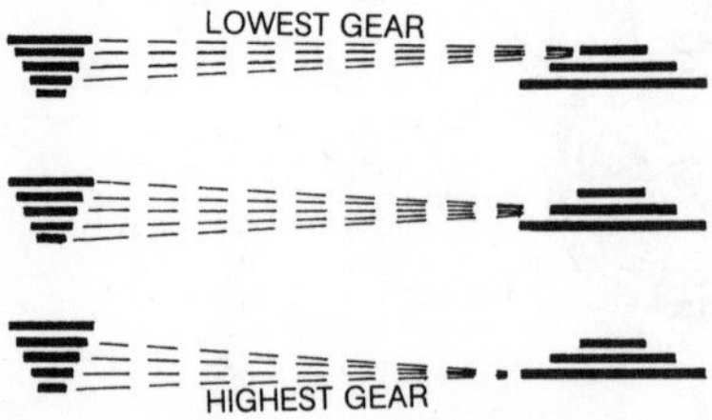

The LH shift lever controls the front changer, which simply shoves the cage through which the chain runs to the left or the right, moving it onto the smaller or the bigger chainring. Pulling the lever back engages the bigger chainring for the higher gear range on most models; pushing it forward engages the smaller chainring, to obtain the lower gearing range.

### The Need for Gears

The reason for gearing lies in the possibility it provides to pedal at an efficient rate with comfortable force under a wide range of different conditions and riding speeds. If the combination of chainring and sprocket size were fixed, as it is on the single-speed bicycle, any given pedaling speed invariably corresponds to a certain riding speed. The rear wheel will be turning at a speed that can be simply calculated by multiplying the pedaling rate with the quotient of chainring and sprocket size (expressed in terms of the numbers of teeth):

$$V_{wheel} = V_{pedal} \times T_{front} / T_{rear}$$

where:

$V_{wheel}$ = wheel rotating speed (RPM)

$V_{pedal}$ = pedaling rate (RPM)

$T_{front}$ = number of teeth, chainring

$T_{rear}$ = number of teeth, sprocket

The actual riding speed depends on this wheel rotating speed and the effective wheel diameter. The effective diameter of a nominal 27 inch or 700 mm wheel is about 680 mm. This results in a riding speed in MPH that can be determined by multiplying the wheel speed in RPM

LOWEST GEAR

HIGHEST GEAR

Fig. 8.2 Gear combinations

by 0.08. These two calculations can be combined to find the riding speed in MPH directly from the pedaling rate and the chainring and sprocket sizes as follows:

MPH $= 0.08 \times v_{pedal} \times T_{front} / T_{rear}$

where:

MPH $=$ riding speed in MPH and the other symbols are as defined above.

To express riding speed in km/h, use the following formula instead:

km/h $= 0.125 \times v_{pedal} \times T_{front} / T_{rear}$

To give an example, assume you are pedaling at a rate of 80 RPM on a bike geared with a 42- tooth chainring and a 21-tooth rear sprocket. Your riding speed, expressed in MPH and km/h respectively, will be:

$0.08 \times 80 \times 42 / 21 = 13$ MPH

$0.125 \times 80 \times 42 / 21 = 20$ km/h

Depending on the prevailing terrain conditions, that may be too easy or too hard for optimum endurance performance. If you are riding up a steep incline, this speed may require a very high pedal force, which may well be too exhausting and damaging to muscles, joints and

tendons. On a level road the same speed will be reached so easily that you don't feel any significant resistance. All right for cruising, but not if you want to get to work on time.

The derailleur gearing system allows you to choose the combination of chainring and sprocket sizes that enables you to operate effectively at your chosen pedaling rate for optimal performance. You may of course also vary the pedaling rate, which would appear to have the same effect as selecting another gear. Indeed, with any given gear, pedaling slower reduces riding speed and therefore demands less power, whereas a higher pedaling rate increases road speed, requiring more power.

However, power output is not the sole, nor indeed the most important, criterion. Performing work at a given level of power output may tax the body differently depending on the associated forces and speeds of movements. It has been found that to cycle longer distances effectively, without tiring or hurting excessively, the pedal force must be kept down by pedaling at a rate well above

Shimano Deore XT rear derailleur with indexed shifters for use on mountain bikes or hybrids. All indexed systems work, this one perfectly. Highly recommended for commuting purposes.

what seems natural to the beginning cyclist.

Whereas the beginner tends to plod along at 40—60 RPM, efficient long distance cycling requires pedaling rates of 80 RPM and more, while racers generally pedal even faster. That doesn't come overnight, because the cyclist first has to learn to move his legs that fast, but it is an essential requirement for efficient cycling. Much of your early practice should therefore be aimed at mastering the art of pedaling faster. That must be done in a rather low gear.

### Gearing Practice

Once you know that high gears mean big chainrings and small sprockets, it's time to get some practice riding in high and low gears. First do it 'dry': the bike supported with the rear wheel off the ground. Turn the cranks by hand and use the shift levers to change up and down, front and rear, until you have developed a good idea of the combinations reached in all conceivable shift lever positions. Listen for rubbing and crunching noises as you shift, realizing a shift has not been executed properly until the noises have subdued. This may mean you have to adjust the lever a little one way or the other until all is quiet.

Now take to the road. Select a stretch of quiet road, where you can experiment around with your gears without risk of being run into the ground by a closely following vehicle or get in the way of other cyclists. Start off in a low gear and shift the rear derailleur up in steps. Then shift to another chainring and change down through the gears with the rear derailleur — followed by the third chainring if your bike has an 18- or 21- speed system.

Reduce the pedal force, still pedaling forward as you shift. Especially the front derailleur will not shift as smoothly as it did when the cranks were turned by hand. You will notice that the noises become more severe and that some changes just don't take place as you had intended. On a bike without index gearing, you may have to overshift slightly first: push the lever a little beyond the correct position to affect a definite change, and then back up until the chain is quiet again. Get a feel for each gear and try to imagine which gear you should select for any given set of conditions. Practice shifting until it goes smoothly and naturally.

Occasionally, it may be necessary to fine-tune the front derailleur position after a change with the rear derailleur. That will be the case when the chain is twisted under an angle that causes it to rub against the side of the front changer. Some people never learn, quite simply

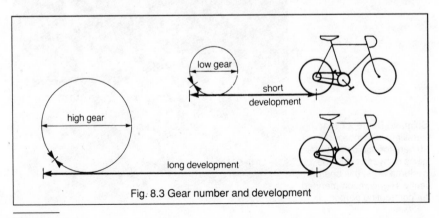

Fig. 8.3 Gear number and development

because they don't take the trouble to practice consciously. Others take that trouble and learn to shift predictably and smoothly within a week. Half an hour of intensive practice each day during one week, and the continued attention required to do it right during regular riding, is all it takes to become an expert very quickly.

In recent years most manufacturers have introduced indexed derailleur systems with matching freewheel blocks that eliminate the need for fine-tuning. These indexed systems, such as the Shimano SIS and SunTour Accushift, work very well when new. However, a slight misalignment or a little wear can play havoc with the indexing of the various gears. In that case, just move

Luxury derailleur: Campagnolo's top of the line Super Record model. Though fine for narrow-range gearing, most commuters will probably find the modern Japanese (or even some of the other European) indexed derailleurs at less than half the price more to their liking.

the auxiliary lever to the F-position and use as a non-indexed model until you can get it readjusted at the bike shop.

## Gear Designation

Just how high or low any given gear is may be expressed by giving the respective numbers of teeth on chainring and sprocket engaged in the particular gear. However, this is not a very good measure. It may not be immediately clear that a combination designated 42 X 16 has the same effect as one designated 52 X 21. Yet they really do result in the same ratio, as can be verified mathematically. It will be clear that it becomes nearly impossible to compare gears on bikes with different wheel sizes this way. There must be a better method.

To allow a direct comparison between the gearing effects of different gears and bikes, two methods are in use, referred to as gear number and development, respectively, and illustrated in Fig. 8.3. Gear number is a somewhat archaic method, used mainly in the English speaking world. It is the equivalent wheel size in inches of a directly driven wheel that corresponds to any given combination of wheel size, chainring and sprocket. It is determined by multiplying the quotient of chainring and sprocket sizes with the wheel diameter in inches:

gear $= D_{wheel} \times T_{front} / T_{rear}$

where:

gear $=$ gear number in inches

$D_{wheel} =$ wheel diameter in inches

$T_{front} =$ number of teeth, chainring

$T_{rear} =$ number of teeth, sprocket

Returning to the example for a bike with 27-inch wheels, geared with a 42-tooth chainring and a 21-tooth sprocket, the gear number would be:

gear $= 27 \times 42 / 21 = 54$ in

This is the customary, though rather quaint method used in the English speaking world to define bicycle gearing. The rest of the world expresses the gear in terms of development. That is the distance in meters covered by the bike with one crank revolution. Development is calculated as follows:

Dev.   $= 3.14 \times d_{wheel} \times T_{front} / T_{rear}$

where:

Dev.      = development in m

$d_{wheel}$   = wheel size in m

$T_{front}$    = number of teeth, chainring

$T_{rear}$    = number of teeth, sprocket

The development for the same example would be:

Dev. $= 3.14 \times 0.680 \times 42 / 21 = 4.30$ m

In practice, you are not expected to figure this kind of thing out yourself. Instead, you may refer to the tables in the Appendix. Just remember that a high gear is expressed by a high gear number or a 'long' development. For a typical commuting situation, low gears are in the lower thirties (around 2.80—3.20 m in terms of development). High gears are those above 90 in (development over 7.20 m).

### Gear Selection

Possibly the biggest problem for the beginning cyclist is to determine which is the right one out of the bewildering array of available gears. To generalize for most normal cycling conditions, I would say it's whichever gear allows you to maximize your pedaling rate without diminishing your capacity to do effective work.

Perhaps you start off with the ability to pedal no faster than 60 RPM. That'll be too slow once you have absolved some riding practice, but for now that may be your limit. So the right gear is the one in which you can reach that rate at any time, preferably exceeding it. Count it

out with the aid of a wrist watch (or with the pedaling rate device incorporated in some bicycle computers). If you find yourself pedaling slower, change down into a slightly lower gear, to increase the pedaling rate at the same riding speed. If you're pedaling faster, keep it up until you feel you are indeed spinning too lightly, and only then change into a slightly higher gear to increase road speed at the same pedaling rate.

Gradually, you will develop the ability to pedal faster. As that happens, increase the limiting pedaling rate along with your ability, moving up from 60 to 70, 80 and eventually even higher pedaling rates.

It should not take too long before you learn to judge the right gear in advance, without the need to count out the pedal revolutions. You will not only know to change down into a lower gear when the direction of the road changes to expose you to a head wind or when you reach an incline, you will also learn to judge just how far to change down — and up again when the conditions become more favorable. Change gear consciously and frequently in small steps, and you will soon enough master the trick

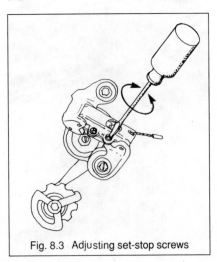

Fig. 8.3  Adjusting set-stop screws

## Derailleur Care and Adjustment

For optimal operation of the derailleur system, several things should be regularly checked and adjusted when necessary. The derailleurs themselves, as well as the chain and the various sprockets, chainrings and control cables, must be kept clean and lightly lubricated. The cables must be just taut when the shift levers are pushed forward and the derailleurs engage the appropriate gear. The tension screw on the shift levers must be kept tightened to give positive shifting without being excessively tight or loose.

When the chain gets shifted beyond the biggest or smallest chainring or sprocket, or when certain combinations

This is what happens as you change gear with the rear derailleur: the chain is simply shoved over sideways to engage the next bigger or smaller sprocket.

can not be reached, the derailleurs themselves must be adjusted. For this purpose they are equipped with set-stop screws, which can be adjusted with a small screwdriver, as illustrated in Fig. 8.4. If necessary, first place the chain back on the sprocket or chainring. To adjust the derailleur, proceed as follows:

*Adjust Derailleur*

**1.** Establish where the problem lies: front or rear derailleur, shifted too far or not far enough, on the inside or the outside.

**2.** Determine which of the set-stop screws governs movement limitation in the appropriate direction. On many models these screws are marked with H and L for high and low gear, respectively. If not, establish yourself which is the appropriate screw by observing what happens at the ends of the screws as you shift towards the extreme gears. The high range set-stop screw is the one towards which an internal protrusion moves as you shift into the highest gear with the appropriate shifter.

**3.** Unscrew the set-stop screw slightly (perhaps half a turn at a time) to increase the range if the extreme gear could not be reached. Tighten it if the chain was shifted beyond that last sprocket.

**4.** Check all possible combinations to establish whether the system works properly, and fine-tune if necessary.

## Derailleur Capacity

Not all derailleurs are capable of handling all possible combinations of gears. As this subject is very complicated, due to the vast array of different makes, models, sizes and combinations of front and rear derailleurs, sprockets and chainrings, it will be impossible to do more than alert you to the problem.

Before selecting any uncommon combination, ask in the bike store whether it will work with the equipment you already have on the bike — or intend to install to replace what you have.

In addition to the conventional systems with simple round chainrings, there are some systems on the market that differ. Of the various types that have been introduced from time to time, so far the most prominent is the Shimano Biopace system, installed on virtually all mountain bikes and sports bikes today.

The Biopace system uses curiously shaped off-round chainrings, available to match the same manufacturer's cranksets. Like all non-standard systems, the Biopace seems to bring an advantage only to those cyclists who have not learned to pedal at a high rate in a relatively low gear. The chainring sizes available for this system are somewhat limited. Nice equipment, but it will be smarter to get used to spinning fast and smoothly, using conventional equipment, selecting your gears consciously.

# 9. Advanced Riding Skills

In the present chapter we will take a closer look at the skills needed to cycle effectively and safely. Though other cyclists — be they racers or tourists — also have to master similar skills, there are some special aspects to consider for cycling in an urban environment, which will be emphasized here wherever appropriate.

The first section of this chapter will deal with honing your skills of riding the bicycle competently, with proper control over the steering and braking systems. This will help you cycle with minimal effort and maximum confidence. In the next section you will be introduced to the peculiarities of effective riding techniques for cycling at speed. Although an understanding of the theoretical background is helpful, I shall concentrate as much as possible on the practical aspects, making you practice what you learn.

### Looking Back and One-Handed Riding

More than in any other form of cycling, these are essential skills for the bicycle commuter. They should be practiced before proceding to any other, more complex, skills. In traffic, the only way to survive is by checking behind you to make sure the coast is clear before you leave your present position in the road, as will be explained more fully in Chapter 12.

First practice riding single-handed on an empty parking lot or in another safe place. Sit relatively upright at first and let go of the left hand, making a conscious effort to continue riding a straight line. Then do the same with the right hand. Next, practice steering the bike single-handed around curves and corners.

While holding the handlebars with the right hand only, look over your left shoulder at the road behind you. It's best to do this with another cyclist, so you can take turns riding in front, while the cyclist in the rear puts up a hand with a certain number of fingers stretched out. Look behind and say how many fingers were raised. Then do the same looking over the right shoulder. Finally, do these same exercises keeping both hands on the handlebars. These practice sesions should perhaps be continued daily for about a week, until you are completely at ease looking behind and riding while holding the handlebars with only one hand. Once you can do it going straight, also practice doing it in curves.

Curve radius, speed and lean are inter-related. At higher speed, more lean in the direction of the turn is required. The figure in the center follows the natural curve. To force a tighter curve at a low speed, lean the bike more than the body. To force a tighter curve at high speed, lean the body more than the bike.

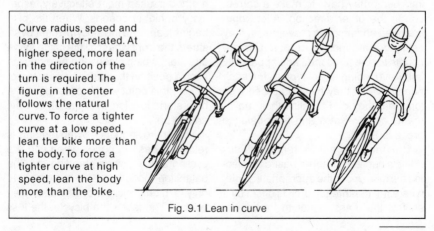

Fig. 9.1 Lean in curve

## The Steering Principle

A bicycle is not steered most effectively by merely turning the handlebars and following the front wheel, as is the case for any two-track vehicle, such as a car. Though bicycles and other single-track vehicles indeed follow the front wheel, they also require the rider to lean his vehicle into the curve to balance it at the same time.

If you were to merely turn the handlebars, the lower part of the bike would start running away from its previous course in the direction in which the front wheel is then pointed, while the mass of the rider, perched high up on the bike, would continue following the original course due to inertia. Thus, the center of gravity would not be in line with the supporting bike, and the rider would come crashing to the ground. Due to the effect of centrifugal force, the tendency to throw the rider off towards the outside of the curve increases with higher speeds, requiring a more pronounced lean the faster you are going.

It is possible to steer by turning the handlebars, and then correcting lean and steering to regain balance afterwards. In fact, many older people, especially women, seem to do it that way, succeeding quite well at low speeds only. As soon as imbalance becomes imminent, they have to make a correction in the other direction. After some cramped and anxious movements, they finally get around the corner. This accounts for the tensioned and apparently impulsive riding style typical for such riders, even if they have practiced it so long that they don't realize their movements are awkward and their balance precarious.

The more effective technique for riding a curve at speed is based on placing the bike under the appropriate angle, where the centrifugal force is offset by a shift of the mass center to the inside,

before turning off. Two methods may be used, depending on the amount of time and room available to carry out the maneuver. I refer to these two methods as natural and forced turn, respectively. To understand either, we should first take a look at the intricacies of balancing the bike when riding a straight line, after which the two methods of turning can be explained.

### Bicycle Balance

What keeps a bicycle or any other single track vehicle going without falling over is the inertia of its moving mass. Rolling a narrow hoop will show that it is an unstable balance: once the thing starts to lean either left or right, it will just go down further and further until it hits the ground. That's because the mass is no longer supported vertically in line with the force. Try it with a bicycle wheel if you like. If the bike's front wheel could not be steered and the rider couldn't move sideways, he'd come down the same way very soon.

On the bicycle, the rider feels when the vehicle starts to lean over. Theoretically, there are two ways out of the predicament: either move the rider back over the center of the contact between bike and road, or move the bike back under the rider. In practice, the latter method is used most effectively, especially at higher speeds. When the bike begins leaning to the side, the rider oversteers the front wheel a little in the same direction, which places the bike back in such a position that balance is restored. In fact, this point will be passed, so the bike starts leaning over the other way, and so on.

This entire sequence of movements is relatively easy to notice when you are cycling slowly. When standing still, the balancing motions are so extreme that only a highly skilled cyclist can keep control. The faster the bicycle, the less perceptible (though equally important) are the steering corrections required to retain balance. To get an understanding of this whole process, I suggest you practice riding a straight line at a low speed. Then do it at a higher speed, and see whether you agree with the explanation, referring also to Fig. 9.1.

Both riding a straight line and staying upright with the bike are merely illusions. In reality, the bike is always in disequilibrium, following a more or less curved track. The combination of bike with rider leans alternately one way and the other. At higher speeds the curves are longer and gentler, while the amount of lean can be perceptible; at lower speeds the curves are shorter and sharper, with less pronounced lean angles for any given deviation.

## The Natural Turn

Under normal circumstances, the rider knows well ahead where to turn off, and there is enough room to follow a generously wide curve. This is the situation of the natural turn. It makes use of the lean that results from normal straight path steering corrections. To turn to the right naturally, you simply wait until the bike is leaning over that way, while the

left turn is initiated when the bike is leaning to the left.

Instead of turning the handlebars to that same side, as would be done to get back in balance to ride straight, you just leave the handlebars alone for a while. This causes the bike to lean over further and further in the direction of the turn. Only when the lean is quite significant, do you steer in the same direction, but not as abruptly as you would do to get back up straight. Instead, you fine-tune the ratio of lean and steering deflection to ride the curve out.

When the turn is completed, you will still be leaning over in the direction of the turn, and you would ride a circle without some other corrective action on your part. You get back on the straight course by steering further into the curve than the amount of lean demands to maintain your balance. This puts your mass center back right above the bike or even further over, allowing you to resume the slightly curving course with which you approximate the straight line. This is illustrated in Fig. 9.2.

Chances are you learned to do this subconsciously when you were a kid, but never realized that you were doing all this. You could perhaps continue to ride a bicycle forever without under-

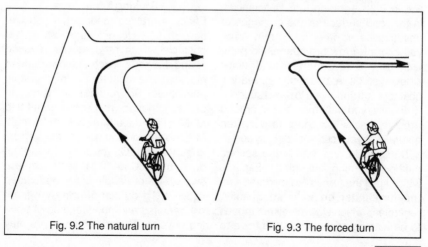

Fig. 9.2 The natural turn          Fig. 9.3 The forced turn

standing the theory. However, to keep control over the bike in demanding situations encountered while riding fast in difficult terrain, you will be much better off if you have the theoretical knowledge and have learned to ride a calculated course, making use of this information. Get a feel for it by riding around an empty parking lot many times, leaning this way and that, following straight lines and making turns, until it is both second nature and something you can do consciously, knowing the relevant limitations.

While you are practicing this technique, as well as when riding at other times, note that speed, curve radius, lean and load are all closely correlated. A sharper turn requires more lean at any given speed. At a higher speed, any given curve requires greater lean angles than the same curve radius at a lower speed. Finally, a loaded bike tends to lean more than an unloaded machine. As you practice this technique, learn to judge which are the appropriate combinations under different circumstances.

### The Forced Turn

You will often be confronted with situations that don't allow you to wait until you are conveniently leaning the appropriate way to make a gradual turn. Deficiencies in the road surface or the presence of obstructions or other traffic may force you into a narrow predetermined path, with only a few inches to deviate sideways. Or a suddenly appearing obstacle may force you to divert suddenly. Finally, you may have to get around a curve that is too sharp to be taken naturally at your current riding speed.

These situations require the second method of turning, illustrated in Fig. 9.3, which I call the forced turn. In this case, the turn must be initiated quickly, regardless which way the bike happens to be leaning at the time. You have to

force the bike to lean over in the appropriate direction and under the right angle consistent with the direction and radius of the turn. And it has to be done quickly.

Do that by sharply steering *away* from the turn just before you get there. You and the bike will immediately start to lean over in the direction of the turn. You have very quickly achieved a considerable lean angle in the direction of the turn. This must be compensated by steering quite abruptly in the same direction. Since this is the direction of the turn, you are set up just right to make a sharp turn. Once completed, steer back into the turn just a little further, to get the lean for regaining the roughly straight course, as explained for the natural turn.

The forced turn technique should be practiced intensively and consciously, since it by no means comes naturally. Initiating a left turn by steering right will probably require the beginning cyclist to overcome all sorts of reasonable inhibitions and demands lots of practice. Take your bike to a grassy area or an empty parking lot a few days in a row, wearing protective clothing in case you fall: helmet, gloves, jacket and long pants.

### Braking Technique

Effective braking means that you can ride up fast close to the turn or the obstacle which requires the reduced speed, brake to reach the lower speed quickly, and accelerate immediately afterwards. So you will be using the brakes to get down in speed from 30 to 20 MPH to take a turn, or from 30 to 28 MPH to avoid running into the vehicle ahead of you. Or you may have to get down from 50 to 10 MPH to handle a switchback or hairpin curve on a steep descent. To do that effectively without risk requires an understanding of braking physics. Though at times you may have to reduce speed quickly, you should also develop a feel for gradual speed reduction to prevent skidding and loss of control. In fact, most cyclists are more often in danger due to braking too vigorously than due to insufficient stopping power.

Braking amounts to deceleration, or speed reduction, which can only take place more or less gradually. The rate of deceleration can be measured and is expressed in $m/sec^2$. A deceleration of 1 $m/sec^2$ means that after each second of braking the traveling speed is 1 m/sec less than it was at the beginning of that second. A speed of 30 MPH corresponds to 13 m/sec. To get down to standstill would take 13 sec if the braking deceleration is 1 $m/sec^2$; it would take 4 seconds to reach 9 m/sec, or 20 MPH. At a higher rate of deceleration it would take less time (and a shorter distance) to get down to the desired speed.

The modern bicycle has remarkably effective brakes, providing it's not raining. In dry weather, a modest force on the brake lever can cause a deceleration of 4—5 $m/sec^2$ with just one brake. Applying both brakes, the effect is even more dramatic, enabling you to slow down from 30 to 15 MPH within one second. There are some factors that limi just how vigorously you can brake on the

bike, even with the best brakes available, though.

In the first place, rain has a negative effect on the rim brake's performance, as the build-up of water reduces the friction between brake block and rim drastically. This applies especially if the bike is equipped with ordinary rubber brake blocks, as offered by most manufacturers as standard equipment. With any rubber brake blocks, I measured a reduction from 4.5 to 2.0 $m/sec^2$ for a given lever force (and to half that figure for bicycles with chrome plated steel rims, which should therefore not be used, even on the cheap bicycles on which they are installed). Lately, some special brake block materials have been introduced that are less sensitive to rain.

The second restriction is associated with a change in the distribution of weight between the wheels as a result of braking. Because the mass center of the rider is quite high above the road, and its horizontal distance to the front wheel axle comparatively small, the bicycle has a tendency to tip forward in response to deceleration. Weight is transferred from the rear to the front of the bike, as illustrated in Fig. 9.4. When the deceleration reaches about 3.5 $m/sec^2$, the weight on the rear wheel is no longer enough to provide traction,

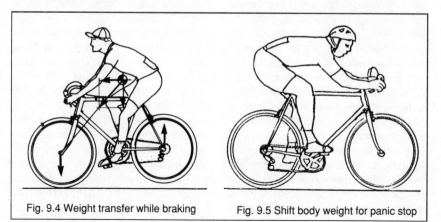

Fig. 9.4 Weight transfer while braking        Fig. 9.5 Shift body weight for panic stop

and the contact between tire and road is reduced to zero. Braking harder than that with the rear brake just makes the rear wheel skid, resulting in loss of control.

In a typical riding posture, the rear wheel actually starts to lift off the ground when a deceleration of about 6.5 m/sec$^2$ is reached, whether using both brakes together or the front brake alone. Consequently, no conventional bicycle can ever be decelerated beyond this limit, regardless of the kind, number and quality of the brakes. This is a very high deceleration, which you should not often reach, but it is good to realize there is such a limit and that it can not be avoided by using the rear brake either alone or in addition to the front brake, but only by braking less vigorously. During a sudden speed reduction or panic stop such high decelerations may be reached. In such cases, reduce the toppling-over effect by shifting your body weight back and down as much as possible: sit far back and hold the upper body horizontally, as illustrated in Fig. 9.5.

Since about twice as great a deceleration is possible with the front brake as with the one in the rear, the former should preferably be used under normal conditions. In most circumstances short of a panic stop or braking in a curve, you can brake very effectively using the front brake alone. When both brakes are used simultaneously, the one in the front can be applied quite a bit harder than the one in the rear. If you notice the rear brake is less effective if pressed equally far, it will be time to check, and if necessary adjust, lubricate or replace the brake cable.

Of course, most braking is not done abruptly, so gradual braking must also be practiced. In particular when the road is slick, in curves or when others are following closely behind, gradual decelera-

tion and the ability to control the braking force within narrow limits is of vital importance. Practice braking consciously with utmost attention to the complex relationship between initial speed, brake lever force and deceleration, to become fully competent at handling the bike when slowing down under all conceivable circumstances.

Braking becomes a different kettle of fish in hilly terrain. On a steep downhill, the slope not only increases the tendency to tip forward, it also induces an accelerating effect, which must be overcome by the brakes even to merely keep the speed constant. A 10% slope induces an acceleration of about 1 m/sec$^2$. Obviously, you will encounter big problems in wet weather on such a downhill stretch if you don't keep your speed down to start with. So it will be necessary to reduce the speed by gradual, intermittent braking. This will help wipe most of the water from the rims, retaining braking efficiency a little better. This way, the brakes are not overtaxed when you do have to reduce the speed suddenly, as may be required to handle an unexpected obstacle or a sharp turn.

### Getting up to Speed

Especially for the commuting cyclist, it is important to know how to reach an acceptable speed quickly and smoothly, to keep up with the traffic. In Chapter 7 you have been shown how to get on the bike and start off smoothly. The next trick is to reach the ultimate riding speed as quickly and efficiently as possible. The idea is to waste as little time and energy as possible during this process of getting up to speed. Tricky, because acceleration demands disproportionately high levels of power and consumes energy correspondingly. And the faster it's done, the more demanding it is.

Clearly, you have to strike a balance here. Accelerating faster than necessary wastes energy that will be sorely needed later. Done too slowly, it may become a plodding affair. It will be your decision to find the right balance between speed and power, but the way to reach it is easy to describe: start in a low gear and increase speed gradually but rapidly. No fast and slow spurts but a gradual build-up of speed.

Either keep pedaling faster and faster in the low gear, changing up only as you reach a significant speed, or be prepared to do some short duration hard work, standing on the pedals, pulling on the upstroke, as well as pushing on the downstroke. As soon as speed is reached, sit on the saddle and select a good gear for spinning at a comfortable but high pedaling rate.

### Riding a Constant Speed

Not only does a good cyclist ride the same number of miles one hour as the next, he travels as many yards one minute as the next, as many feet with one crank revolution as the next, and indeed ideally as many inches during each section within any revolution. If you slow down during one short section, it will take disproportionately more time and energy to make up for the loss.

Pay attention to this at all times while cycling. As long as the external conditions don't change drastically, you should make every effort to keep a constant speed and movement. Gauge your speed by means of a bicycle computer, by comparing it to that of other traffic, or using your watch, counting out pedal revolutions and milestones.

### Accelerating

However efficient a constant speed may be, sometimes you will still want to accelerate to a higher speed. In traffic, you may have to accelerate in situations like

getting across an intersection before the light changes or to avoid running into another vehicle crossing your path.

As with getting up to speed in the first place, it is most efficient to increase the speed as gradually as possible. Unless you are already spinning at your highest possible rate, you will find accelerating by increasing pedaling speed more effective than by increasing pedal force in a higher gear. In other words, as long as you can spin faster, it is best to shift down into a slightly lower gear and increase the pedaling rate vigorously. Once you are gathering momentum and are getting close to your maximum spinning speed, shift up and continue to gain speed in the higher gear.

### Riding Against the Wind

At higher speeds or whenever there is a head wind, the effect of air drag on the power needed to cycle is quite significant. Economize on your effort by avoiding the wind resistance as much as possible. Keep your profile low when cycling against the wind. Try to seek out the sheltered parts of the road wherever possible, without exposing yourself to danger.

### Hill Climbing

With some conscious effort, everybody's climbing skills can be improved up to a point; yet some riders are born climbers, while others may have to go uphill slowly all their lives. Just the same, it is an ability that can be learned and developed well enough by the average rider to at least handle all hills you encounter, even if you go up slowly.

Again, a regular motion is most efficient, and that is best mastered by staying seated in a rather low gear. If your regular commute route is a hilly one, equip the bike with wider ratio gearing than for level riding. Just what sizes of sprockets should be installed is up to you, but I'd say 90% of all beginners tend to pick gear ratios that are too high (or, to put it differently, sprockets that are too small). There should be nothing embarrassing about a rear sprocket with 34 teeth and a chainwheel with 36 or even fewer teeth in the back if you live in a very hilly area.

Some bikes, and particularly mountain bikes, are equipped with gears that are low enough to tackle almost any hill without having to get up from the saddle. And on these bikes we sometimes see the other extreme: people riding in gears that are far too low for the circumstances, spinning like mad but getting nowhere fast. Ride in a gear that allows you to spin fast but with noticeable resistance, so your progress is not merely limited by the speed with which you can turn your legs but by total output.

### Climbing out of the Saddle

When the lowest available gear is too high to allow a smoothly spinning leg motion, it is time to shift to another technique. Some riders try to increase the length of the power stroke by means of some hefty ankle twisting, really pushing the leg around at this point. That is an unnecessarily tiring technique, requiring

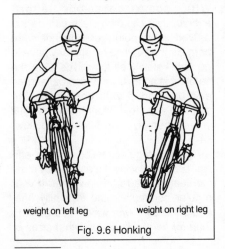

weight on left leg          weight on right leg

Fig. 9.6 Honking

long muscle work phases and short recovery periods. A better method of climbing in a high gear and at a low pedaling speed is referred to as 'honking' in Britain, and seems to be a mystery to most American cyclists.

Honking makes use of the rider's body weight to push down the pedals, while the body is pulled up after each stroke very quickly by standing up. In this mode, the muscle work is done each time the body is raised, rather than when pushing the pedal down and around. To do it effectively, hold the tops of the brake lever mounts in the front of (dropped) handlebars. You can either take quick snappy steps or throw your weight from side to side in a swinging motion, as illustrated in Fig. 9.6. I suggest you practice honking as well as spinning: the one in a high gear at pedaling rates below 55 RPM, the other in a low gear at 65 RPM or more. Avoid pedaling rates of 55—65 RPM by choosing the gearing range to stay within either the one range or the other.

### Avoiding Obstacles

Sometimes you will be confronted with some kind of obstacle right in your path. This may be anything from a pothole or a broken exhaust to a discarded can or bottle. Even when travelling at speed and with little room to maneuver, you can learn to avoid running into such things by using the technique illustrated in Fig. 9.7.

As soon as you perceive the obstacle ahead of you, decide whether to pass it to the left or the right. Fix your sight on the point where you intend to pass, rather than on the obstacle itself. Ride straight up to it and then, before you reach it, briefly but decisively steer into the direction *opposite* to that of your chosen avoidance (to the right if you want to pass on the left). This makes the bike lean over towards the other side (to the left in this case). Now steer in that direction just as quickly, which will result in a very sharp forced turn. As soon as you've passed the obstacle, oversteer a little more, to cause a lean that helps you put the bike back on its proper course.

This kind of maneuver is useful in such situations as crossing a railway track that runs diagonally across the road. Since the front wheel would be likely to get caught in the ridge or the rail, you have to take a course that is as perpendicular to it as possible. Besides, you have to stay upright when doing so, in order to avoid slipping sideways. Achieve both by moving over sideways well before you reach it, then ride your

curve towards it, and cross it perpendicularly. See the comments in Chapter 12 for making sure to avoid being run down by following vehicles when doing this.

This too is something to practice on an empty parking lot, wearing a helmet and two long sleeved shirt (the double layer of fabric is much easier on the skin, since the one layer will just slip off the other, rather than removing chunks of your flesh). Mark phoney obstacles with chalk or place foam pads or sponges on the pavement, and practice passing them abruptly on both sides until you master the trick.

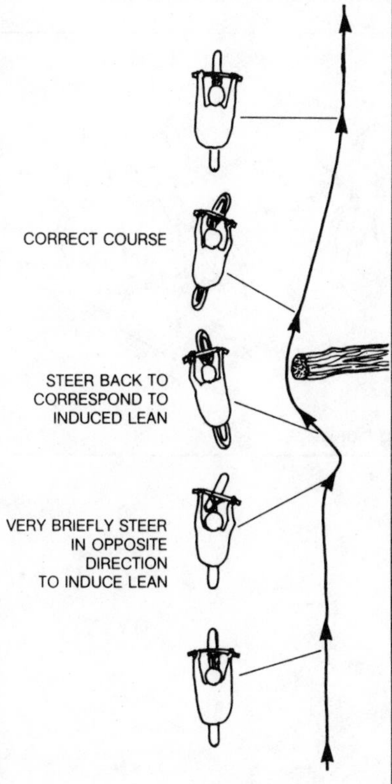

### Jumping the Bike
Another useful act for hard riding situations is the skill of making first the front, then the rear wheel jump over an obstacle. You may have to do that when there is an unavoidable obstacle ahead of you. It's a matter of shifting your weight back or forth to lift the appropriate wheel off the ground. To jump up, first throw your weight backwards, while pulling up on the handlebars to unload the front wheel while lifting it. At the same time accelerate vigorously by pushing hard on the forward pedal. With some practice, you'll soon be able to lift the front end of the bike at least a foot up in the air.

Next, try to do the same with the rear wheel, throwing your weight forward while pulling up your legs and bottom at the same time. This is harder, but it can also be mastered. Finally, practice coordinating the two shifts, so that you first lift the front and then, as soon as you've reached the highest point, start raising the back. After some time, you should be able to actually make the bike fly: lift both wheels in such short sequence that the rear wheel comes off the ground well before the front wheel comes down.

CORRECT COURSE

STEER BACK TO CORRESPOND TO INDUCED LEAN

VERY BRIEFLY STEER IN OPPOSITE DIRECTION TO INDUCE LEAN

Fig. 9.7 Obstacle avoidance

One variant of this technique is the art of jumping up sideways, which may be needed to handle obstacles like curbs, ridges and — most relevant in bicycle commuting: railway or streetcar tracks that run under a very oblique angle to the road — i.e. almost parallel to it. To do this, the bike has to be forced to move sideways in a short and snappy diversion just preceding the jump. Do that by combining the diversion technique described above under *Avoiding Obstacles* with the jump, as illustrated in Fig. 9.8.

Get close to the ridge you want to jump, riding parallel to it. Then briefly steer away from it. This immediately causes the bike to lean towards the obstacle. Now catch yourself by steering sharply in that same direction, lifting the front wheel when you are close to the obstacle, immediately followed by the rear wheel. Practice is all it takes, and the empty parking lot with a chalk line as a substitute ridge is the best place to do that.

Sometimes you will have to ride through a big pothole, a ditch or any other depression. To do that with minimal risk to bike and rider, you can use something akin to the jumping technique. Enter the depression with your weight near the front of the bike. Then unload the front wheel by throwing your weight back and pulling up the handlebars before the front wheel hits the lowest point of the depression. Finally, ride up the other side and pull up the rear, while shifting your weight to the front of the bike to climb back out.

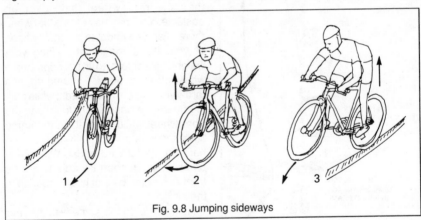

Fig. 9.8 Jumping sideways

# 10. Bicycle Safety

Bicycle commuting is not an entirely riskless undertaking. Neither are many other pursuits, but what scares off potential cyclists most is probably the danger of being involved in a collision with a motor vehicle. Yes, that chance exists in bicycle commuting, as it does when crossing the street in front of your own house. Actually, this is but one of several kinds of possible injury causes in bicycling. You can learn to avoid most of the risks and minimize the impact of these and other injuries and health hazards. These are the subjects of the present chapter and the next one, respectively.

Considering the various risks, ranging from those to your own body and equipment to the harm or loss you may cause others, it may be smart to take out some kind of insurance. Personal liability insurance is perhaps the most important one of these. In addition, you may want to make sure you have adequate health insurance to cover the dangers of the road. This advice may sound exagerated to most non-US readers, and it is not intended for them: in the US a little accident can cost a fortune in liability claims and health care.

## The Risks of Bicycling

Quite a lot of research has been done in recent years on the subject of bicycle accidents and injuries. To summarize the available evidence in a nutshell, the majority of bicycle accidents is attributable to a very limited number of typical mistakes, most of which can be either avoided or counteracted by intelligent cycling techniques.

Probably the most significant finding is that the more experienced cyclists have markedly fewer accidents than those who don't cycle frequently. This is one good argument to try and gain ex-perience and skills as quickly as possible. Following the advice contained in the preceding chapters not only increases the joy, satisfaction and effectiveness of your cycling, it also drastically reduces the risk to which you are exposed.

## Traffic Hazards

Fatal accidents are only a small percentage of all injuries, and numerous quite serious accidents do occur. Though the majority of all injured cyclists themselves are at least partly to blame for their injuries (even if not legally at fault), there always will be some accidents that are directly attributable to bullying and inconsiderate motorists.

Unfortunately, this type of accident forms a high proportion of those that experienced cyclists encounter. These riders have learned to handle their machines rationally and safely in traffic, thus virtually eliminating their risk concerning the more common kinds of accidents to which the incompetent are exposed. Having practically eliminated the latter, they are just as vulnerable to the remaining irrational dangers of the road.

The only defense against inconsiderate road users is not to provoke them. Give in, even if that seems highly unfair. It's an unequal battle and sometimes it's just smarter not to insist on justice. You will encounter relatively few of these particular risks as a commuting cyclist, since you are not likely to be on the road at the times when they are most likely: Sunday afternoons and late evenings, when many boisterous drunks are on the road. Oddly enough, these accidents are also more likely on relatively lightly travelled roads near smaller towns than on typical busy commuting roads near bigger cities.

Most accidents, of course, are not of this type. They simply happen when two people make a mistake each: one initiates a wrong move, and the other fails to react in such a way that a collision is avoided. Keep that in mind when cycling. Remain alert for the possible mistakes others may make, and try to avoid doing the unexpected or unconsidered yourself as much as humanly possible. Anticipate not only the predictable, but also the unexpected: the motorist looming behind the next corner or intersection, the dog suddenly running into the road, the car just as unexpectedly appearing from a driveway, or the idiot bicyclist suddenly crossing your path in the dark without lights.

The latter subject deserves special attention, but the only way to arm yourself is to make sure you do not cycle out after dark without lights yourself, so at least *you* can be seen. Proper lighting on the bike is needed in addition to the curiously ineffective array of reflectors that is increasingly prescribed by law in various countries. The gravest danger of reflectors lies in the inappropriate impression they transmit of your visibility, whereas in reality several of them only make you visible to those who do not endanger you anyway. A bright light in the front and a big rear light or reflector facing back are essential, while all the other goodies won't do a thing that the former wouldn't do more effectively.

Most accidents occur by day, even though the relative risk is greater at night. Whether by day or at night, cycle with all your senses alert. In general, ride your bike as you would drive your car, always verifying whether the road ahead of you is clear, and taking particular care to select your path wisely at junctions and intersections. As a relatively slow vehicle, you must look behind you to ascertain that nobody is following closely before you move over into another traffic lane or away from your previous path.

Forget anything you ever heard about bikes being different from motor vehicles. As a wheeled vehicle, your bike answers to the same laws of physics as does your car. Adhere to the most basic rules of traffic as you learned them to handle a car, and you'll be safe on a bike. No doubt the worst advice ever given to cyclists in many parts of the US is to ride on the side of the road where a pedestrian would go, namely facing traffic. On a bike you *are* the traffic, and you belong on the same side as all other vehicles traveling the same way.

The rules of the road as applied to motor vehicles are based on a logical system that has gradually evolved and works as well for cyclists as it does for motorists. This system works the way it does because it is logical and consistent. If it is dangerous for motorists to do certain things, then it will be at least as dangerous on a bike.

Don't hug the curb but claim your place on the road. Don't dart in and out around parked vehicles and other obstructions along the side of the road. At an intersection, choose your path so that you will not be overtaken by vehicles turning off that are likely to cut across your path. Detailed guidelines specifically applicable to urban traffic situations are outlined in chapters 12 and 13.

The most feared type of bicycle accident is the one that involves being hit from behind. These accidents do happen, and though there is hardly any defense possible to ward them off, it is worth considering that they are characterized by a number of common factors. They invariably occur on otherwise deserted roads, where the attention of motorist and cyclist alike are at a low, since both feel perfectly secure.

Inconspicuous clothing, a low sun, blinding one or both participants, and a lack of the cyclist's awareness, due to tiredness at the end of a long day, are also common features. It may be smart to increase your conspicuity. Wearing brightly visible colors, such as yellow, pink, orange or bright green, may well help others spot you in time to avoid this type of accident.

### Falls and Collisions

Whether or not a motor vehicle is involved, virtually every injury to the cyclist is due to the impact when the cyclist falls off the bike. He either hits the road surface, an object on or along the road, the colliding vehicle or the bike itself. The same skills necessary to prevent traffic accidents involving cars will keep you from experiencing most of the other types of falls and collisions. Be watchful, consider the effects of your own actions, and use the technical skills described in the preceding chapter to divert when the situation becomes threatening.

Four types of falls and collisions can be distinguished, caused by stopping, diverting, skidding and loss of control, respectively. In the following sections, I shall describe these accidents, including a few hints about relevant prevention and impact reduction methods.

### Stopping Accidents

In a stopping accident, the bicycle runs into an obstacle that halts its progress. Depending on the cyclist's speed, the impact can be very serious. As the bicycle itself is stopped, inertia keeps the rider going forward, throwing him against or over the handlebars. The kinetic energy of the moving mass will be dissipated very suddenly, often in an unfortunate location. Your genitals may hit the handlebar stem or your skull may crash into something solid.

The way to guard yourself against these accidents is to look and think ahead, so you don't run into any obstacles. If necessary, control your speed to allow handling the unexpected when a potential danger may be looming up behind the next corner. Learn to apply the diverting technique described in Chapter 9. The way to minimize the impact of the most serious form of stopping accident is by wearing an energy absorbing helmet, which will be discussed more fully in Chapter 11.

### Diverting Accidents

A diverting type accident occurs when the front wheel is pushed sideways by an external force, while the rider is not leaning in the same direction to regain balance. Typical causes are railway tracks, cracks in the road surface or the edge of the road. The effect is that you fall sideways and hit the road or some obstacle by the side of the road. Depending how unexpectedly it happened, you may be able to reduce the effect of the fall by stretching out an arm, which seems to be an automatic reflex in this situation.

Characteristic injuries range from abrasions and lacerations of the hands and the sides of arms and legs to bruised hips and sprained or broken wrists. More serious cases, usually incurred at higher speeds, may involve broken collarbones and injuries to the face or the side of the skull. The impact of the lesser injuries can be minimized by wearing padded gloves and double layers of clothing with long sleeves and legs. Wearing a helmet will minimize damage to the side of the head.

Diverting accidents can often be avoided if the cyclist is both careful and alert. Keep an eye out for the typical danger situations. Don't approach surface ridges under a shallow angle. A last second diversion can often be made along the lines of the diverting technique described in Chapter 9. In the case of a ridge in the road surface, use the technique of sideways jumping, also de scribed there.

## Skidding Accidents

When the bicycle keeps going or goes in an unintended direction, despite your efforts to brake or steer, it will be due to skidding between the tires and the road surface. This kind of thing happens more frequently when the road is slick on account of moisture, frost, loose sand or fallen leaves. Especially under these conditions, sudden diversions or movements, hard braking and excessive lean when cornering may all cause skidding.

Skidding accidents often also cause the cyclist to fall sideways, resulting in abrasions, lacerations or, more rarely, fractures. Prevent these by checking the road surface ahead and avoiding sudden steering or braking maneuvers and excessive leaning in curves. Cross slick patches, ranging from wet or greasy asphalt to railway tracks, from sand or leaves on the road to the white lines used as road markings, with the bicycle upright. Achieve that by carrying out the requisite steering and balancing actions *before* you reach such danger spots.

If you can not avoid it, once you feel you are entering a skid, try to move your weight towards the back of the bike as much as possible, sliding back on the saddle and stretching the arms. Follow the bike, rather than trying to force it back. Finally, don't do what seems an obvious reaction to the less experienced, namely getting off the saddle to straddle the top tube with one leg dangling.

## Loss of Control Accidents

At higher speeds, especially in a steep descent, loss of control accidents sometimes occur. In this case, you just can't steer the bike the way you intend to go. This happens when you find yourself having to steer in one direction at a time when you are leaning the other way, or when speed control braking initiates unexpected oscillations. Often this situation develops into a collision or a fall along the lines of one of the other accident types described above.

Prevention is only possible with experience: don't go faster than the speed at which you feel in control. The more you ride under various conditions, the more you will develop a feel for what is a safe speed, when to brake and how to steer to maintain control over the bike. Once the situation sets in, try to keep your cool. Don't panic. Follow the bike, rather than forcing it over. The worst thing you can do is to tense up and get off the saddle. Stay in touch with handlebars, seat and pedals, and steer in the direction of your lean. This way, you may well get out of it without falling or colliding, though your nerves may have suffered somewhat.

# 11. Bicycling Health

In this chapter we shall look at the other side of the safety coin: what to do to treat or avoid injuries and other health hazards associated with cycling. Most of these things are not particularly dangerous, but incorrect treatment can aggravate things, and this chapter will help you minimize this risk.

### Treating Abrasions

Abrasions, referred to as *'road rash'* in club cycling circles, are the most common cycling injury resulting from any kind of fall. They usually heal relatively fast, though they can be quite painful. Wash out the wound with water and soap, and remove any particles of road dirt to prevent infection. Apply a dressing only if the location is covered by clothing, since the wound will heal faster when exposed to the air. Avoid the formation of a scab by treating the wound with an antibbacterial salve.

See a doctor if any signs of infection occur, such as swelling, itching or fever. There may be a risk of tetanus if the wound draws blood. If you have been immunized against tetanus before, get a tetanus shot within 24 hours only if the last one was more than two years ago. If you have never been immunized before, get a full immunization, consisting of two shots within 24 hours, followed by two more after two weeks and six months, respectively.

### Sprained Limbs

In case of a fall, your tendency to stick out an arm to break the impact may result in a sprained or even a fractured wrist. In other accident situations this can also happen to the knee or the ankle. Spraining is really nothing but damage to the ligaments that surround and hold the various parts of a joint together. Typical symptoms are a local sensation of heat, itching and swelling.

Whenever possible, keep the area cold with an ice bag. If you feel a stinging pain or if fever develops, get medical advice, because it may actually be a fracture that was at first incorrectly diagnosed as a sprain. This may be the case when the fracture takes the form of a simple 'clean' crack without superficially visible deformation of the bone.

### Fractures

Typical cycling fractures are those of the wrist and the collarbone, both caused when falling: the one when extending the arm to brake the fall, the other when you don't have time to do that. You or medical personnel may not at first notice a clean fracture as described above: there may be one without any outward sign.

If there is a stinging pain when the part is moved or touched, I suggest you get an X-ray to make sure, even if a fracture is not immediately obvious. You'll need medical help to set and bandage the fractured location, and you must give up cycling until it is healed, which will take about five weeks.

### Head Injuries

If you fall on your head, the impact may smash the brain against the inside of the skull, followed by the reverse action as it bounces back. The human brain can usually withstand this kind of treatment without lasting damage if the resulting deceleration does not exceed about 300 G, or 3000 m/sec$^2$. Look at it this way: the head probably falls to the ground from a height of 1.5 m (5 ft). This results in a speed of 5 m/sec at the time of impact. To keep the deceleration down below 3000 m/sec$^2$, this speed must be reduced to zero in no less than 0.002 sec.

Neither your skull nor the object with which you collide is likely to deform gradually enough to achieve even such a modest kind of cushioning. That's why energy absorbing helmets with thick crushable foam shells were developed. Neither flexible nor rigid materials will do the trick by themselves. It's not a bad idea to have a hard outer shell to distribute the load of a point impact, and it is nice to get some comfort inside from a soft flexible liner, but the crushing of about 2 cm ( $^3/_4$ inch) of seemingly brittle foam is essential to absorb the shock. The minimum requirement for a safe helmet is the American standard ANSI Z-90.4.

To put the brain injury risk in perspective: Consider a big university campus with 4000 cycling students, each riding 5000 miles a year. You would probably know all of them at least by sight. Without helmets, one of them will lose his life each year. If they all wear helmets, fate will only strike once every two or three years. Disagree if you like, but to many of us it is worth wearing that helmet — even if you can do no more than save your own life, which is statistically due after 4000 years of unprotected cycling.

### Other Health Problems

The remaining part of this chapter will be devoted to the health hazards of cycling that have nothing to do with falling off the bike. We will look at the most common complaints and discuss some methods of prevention, as well as possible cures. This brief description can not cover the entire field. Nor should most of the issues discussed here be generalized too lightly. The same symptoms may have different causes in different cases; conversely, the same cure may not work for two superficially similar problems. Yet in most cases the following remarks will apply.

### Saddle Sores

Though beginning bicyclists may at first feel uncomfortable on the bike seat, they have no idea what kind of agony real seat problems can bring. In bicycle commuting, much more than in racing or long distance touring, you have the opportunity to avoid the most serious problems by taking a break from cycling when symptoms start to develop. What happens is that the combined effect of perspiration, pressure and chafing causes cracks in the skin where dirt and bacteria can enter. The result can be anything from a mild inflammation to the most painful boils.

There is of course little chance of these things healing as long as you continue riding vigorously. As soon as any pressure is applied, when you sit on a bike seat, things will get worse. Prevention and early relief are the methods to combat saddle sores. The clue to both is hygiene. Wash and dry both your crotch and your cycling shorts after every day's ride. Many bicyclists also treat the affected area with rubbing alcohol, which both disinfects and increases the skin's resistance to chafing, or with talcum powder, which prevents further damage.

If you wear real cycling gear, you'll need at least two pairs of shorts, so you can always rely on a clean, dry pair when you go out. Wash them out, taking particular care to get the chamois clean, and hang them out to dry thoroughly, preferably outside, where the sun's ultraviolet rays may act to kill any remaining bacteria. Treat the chamois with either talcum powder or a special treatment for that purpose.

The quality of your saddle and your riding position may also affect the development of crotch problems. If early symptoms appear in the form of redness or soreness, consider getting a softer saddle, sitting further to the back of your saddle, or lowering the handlebars a little to reduce the pressure on the seat. If the problem gets out of hand, take a rest from cycling until the sores have fully healed.

### Knee Problems

Because the cycling movement does not apply the high impacting shock loads on the legs that are associated with running, it's surprising that knee problems are so prevalent. They are mainly concentrated with two groups of cyclists: beginners and very strong, muscular riders. In both cases, the cause seems to be pushing too high a gear. This places excessive forces on the knee joint, resulting in damage to the membranes that separate the moving portions of the joint and the ligaments holding the bits and pieces together. In cold weather the problems get aggravated, so it will be wise to wear long pants whenever the temperature is below 18 degrees C (65 degrees F), especially if fast descents are involved.

Prevent excessive forces on the knee joint by gearing so low that you can spin lightly under all conditions, avoiding especially climbing in the saddle with pedaling rates below 60 RPM. Equip your bicycle with gear ratios that allow you to do that, and choose a lower gear whenever necessary. Once the problem has developed, either giving up cycling or riding loosely in low gears will aid the healing process. I suggest you continue cycling in very low gears, spinning freely. That will probably prepare you to get back into shape, while forcing you to avoid the high gears that caused the problem in the first place.

### Tendinitis

This is an infection of the Achilles tendon, which attaches the big muscle of the lower leg, the gastrocnemius, to the heel bone. It is an important tendon in cycling, since the pedaling force can not be applied to the foot without it. It sometimes gets damaged or torn under the same kind of conditions as described above for knee injuries: cycling with too much force in too high a gear. The problem is aggravated by low temperatures, which explains why it generally develops in the early season.

To avoid tendinitis, wear long woollen socks whenever the temperature is below 18 degrees C (65 degrees F). It may also help to wear shoes that come up quite high, maximizing the support they provide. Get used to riding with a supple movement in a low gear, which seems to be the clue to preventing many cycling complaints. Healing requires rest, followed by a return to cycling with minimum pedal force in a low gear.

### Numbness

Especially beginning cyclists, not yet used to riding longer distances, sometimes develop a loss of feeling in certain areas of contact with the bike. The most typical location is the hands, but it also occurs in the feet and the crotch. This is caused by excessive and unvaried prolonged pressure on the nerves and blood vessels. The effects are usually relieved with rest, though they have at times been felt for several days.

Once the problem develops, get relief by changing your position frequently, moving the hands from one part of the handlebars to another, or moving from one area of the seat to another if the crotch is affected. To prevent the numbness in the various locations, use well padded gloves, foam handlebar sleeves, a soft saddle in a slightly higher position, or thick soled shoes with cushioned inner soles, laced loosely at the bottom but tightly higher up, depending on the location of the numbness.

## Back Ache

Many riders complain of aches in the back, the lower neck and the shoulders, especially early in the season. These are probably attributable to insufficient training of the muscles in those locations. It is largely the result of unfamiliar isometric muscle work, keeping still in a forward bent position. This condition may also be partly caused or aggravated by low temperatures, so it is wise to wear warm bicycle clothing in cool weather.

To avoid the early-season reconditioning complaints, the best remedy is not to interrupt cycling in winter. Even if you give up bicycle commuting temporarily, two rides a week at a moderate pace, or the use of a home trainer with a proper low riding position, will do the trick. Alternately, you may start off in the new season with a slightly higher handlebar position and once more a low gear. Sleeping on a firm mattress and keeping warm also seems to either help alleviate or prevent the problem.

## Sinus and Bronchial Complaints

Especially in the cooler periods, many cyclists develop breathing problems, originating either in the sinuses or the bronchi. It is generally attributable to undercooling, the only solution being to dress warmer and to cycle slowly enough to breathe through the nose.

After a demanding climb in cooler weather, do not strip off warm clothing, open your shirt or drink excessive quantities of cold liquids, even if you sweat profusely. All these things cause more rapid cooling than your body may be able to handle. You will cool off gradually and without impairing your health if you merely reduce your output and allow the sweat to evaporate through the fibers of your clothing, especially if it contains a high percentage of wool.

## Sun Burn

When biking, you will be exposed to the sun, particularly on the way home in summer. Unless you have a naturally high resistance to ultra violet light, exposed parts of the body are likely to suffer sun burn, though rarely on the relatively short trips typical for commuting. To prevent it on longer trips, use a sun tan lotion with a protection factor of 15. This means that only one fifteenth of the ultra violet rays reach the skin. Even more effective is zinc oxide based protection, applied in selected locations such as the nose the ears and the neck.

Sun burn is just that: a burn, and that means it should be treated like any other burn. Cold water and perhaps a light dressing, such as baby oil, are all you can do — apart from waiting for it to heal. In really severe cases, sun burn can be serious enough to justify professional medical care. There are substances that suppress the pain, but there is little chance of healing a burn with any kind of treatment.

# Part III
# Bike Commuting as a Way of Life

# 12. The Basics of Cycling in Traffic

Commuting puts the cyclist in a different environment than the one that most people dream of when thinking of bicycling. Most of your riding will be in, or close to, built-up areas and typically you will use busy roads. Not always: in many areas of the world there are surprisingly many options open for the cyclist to use roads that carry little motor traffic at least some of the way.

In this chapter, we shall discuss the basic methods used to be an effective cyclist in traffic. In part, this discussion expands on the material covered in Chapter 10 about safety: it presents the practical lessons learned from the study of the risks of cycling. This material will give you the basic knowledge of traffic to allow you to understand and safely carry out the recommendations that will follow in the next chapter with regards to particular traffic situations.

## Selecting Your Route

Finding a pleasant commuting route is partly a matter of luck — but mainly one of intelligent planning. Get a very detailed map of the area that covers both your home and your destination. Better yet, get two: a regular street map and a topographical map (known as Geological Survey in the US). Comparing the two, and paying particular heed to the difference between them, you may well be able to find a route that is more enjoyable than the first one that comes to mind, certainly if you live in a suburban area.

This method of route finding may also help you discover a route that evens out the hills or avoids other environmental constraints such as strong head winds. There are situations in which a difference in height is most easily taken by pushing up the bike a short section, to enjoy a relatively level ride the rest of the way. Other situations work better when you gradually work your way up, and an equally gradual descend going the other direction. The maps will allow you to spot the alternatives, and it will be your job to try out the different routes in the real world to determine what will work best for you.

In densely built-up areas, on the other hand, the number of possible short-cuts will be limited and their use not always as enjoyable as would at first appear. My short-cuts through San Francisco's Golden Gate Park were both enjoyable and safe on the way to work early in the morning. However, on the way back, throngs of joggers, frisbee-players, picnickers and spaced-out roller skaters turned that route into something that was still more scenic than the main road, but a lot more dangerous.

It is also a mistake to assume that minor roads are less dangerous than major arterials. Not only are the main roads generally wider and designed with safety in mind, they also are protected by means of stop signs and traffic lights — most of which will be working *for* you when you ride along such a road. If you take the minor road that runs just one or two blocks over, every junction will have a stop sign or a traffic light that is timed *against* you. That makes such a road both more time consuming and more dangerous for the cyclist — too high a price to pay for a quieter ride.

I have on one occasion done a very thorough analysis of two such alternative routes. Following the minor road, the number of obstructions (red traffic lights, stop signs, etc.) was more than four times as high as it was on the main road. And what was at least as bad, the time needed to travel along the minor road was nearly 40% more than what was required on the main road — assuming the cyclist followed all the rules of the road conscientiously.

That, one is tempted not to do on a minor road. Even the few law-and-order cyclists I know fall into running stop signs and other illegal practices when they are confronted with too many of them, as they are on any urban minor road. That's not only illegal, but dangerous as well, with the added disadvantage that in case of an accident you will be at fault. This exposes you to unforeseen liability risks, while giving you little hope of recovering any expenses of your own. All that in addition to the greater risk of getting hurt.

### Riding in Traffic
Except for nutrition and astrology, there is probably no subject about which more nonsense has been written than bicycling in traffic. I will not touch upon the two former subjects, but I may have to talk seriously about the latter — fortunately, because it's the only one of the three in which I can claim some expertise. Not much fun, perhaps, but sorely needed if you are to enjoy bicycle commuting and live to tell your children and grand children about it.

The biggest problem so far is that, especially in the US, the presumed difference between bikes and motor vehicles has been emphasized beyond all proportion, ignoring the fact that bikes and cars are all wheeled vehicles following the same laws of physics and driven by people whose minds tick the same

way. Whenever you are confronted with a situation you can't handle right off, think what you would do if you were driving a car. In most cases, that will get you off safely. In Chapter 13, I shall describe individual situations in some detail. Basic to all this are two things: choosing your position and thinking ahead.

Take the peculiarities of other traffic participants into account. I shall be referring to the unpredictability of pedestrians elsewhere. But other cyclists are often at least as unpredictable — part of the inheritance of cycling as an immature activity.

Motorist aren't all blameless either. Their most typical mistake as they interact with bicyclists is to think of them as fixed objects. Once a motorist has overtaken a bike, he assumes it to have disappeared for good. He doesn't realize the cyclist is still there, right next to him or only a very short distance behind, and traveling at such a speed that a sudden stop or diverting maneuver is impossible. Keep that in mind when you are overtaken just before a junction or driveway to the right: chances are the motorist will turn off right in front of you. Drop back whenever there is the slightest risk of this happening

### Primary and Secondary Positions
Elementary to safe and predictable cycling is that *you* have to keep control of the situation. The oldest premise of traffic, namely that the road belongs to who is using it, applies here too: *you* decide where you ride and when it is safe to allow someone else to overtake you. That, you do by choosing the right position in the road.

The correct path depends on the width of the road or the particular traffic lane in which you are. Two different situations apply:

*       Wide lanes are those that are safe for cyclists and motorists next to one

another sharing the same lane. Normally that means at least 4 m (13 ft) lane width.

*    Narrow lanes are those too narrow for safe continuous parallel movement of cars and cyclists. Those are lanes less than 4 m (13 ft) wide.

On each type of lane, a primary and a secondary position can be identified, as illustrated in Fig. 12.1. Whatever the lane width, the primary position is near the middle of the lane. Depending on the situation with respect to traffic speed and density, you may spend most or little of your time in this position, but always think of it as your primary position, because it is the one from which you have control over the situation.

The secondary position is further over to the right. It is used when you decide it is safe to be overtaken. On a wide lane, it is about 1.50 m (5 ft) to the right of the center of the motorist's normal path in that lane. It allows overtaking by a car that only moves over to the left by a few feet, which does not force him to move over into the next lane.

On a narrow lane, the secondary position is between 60 cm and 90 cm (2 ft and 3 ft, respectively) from the RH edge. In this case, cars ovetaking you may have to infringe slightly on the next lane over.

On lanes that vary in width, you should orient yourself on the basis of the path taken by cars, rather than by the momentary width of the lane, to avoid getting trapped when the road narrows again. The same applies where vehicles are parked by the side or where other obstructions narrow the road frequently: don't dart in and out, but claim your place in the lane (see Fig. 12.2).

In addition to the position relative to the cross section of the lane, the other consideration is which lane to choose when the road has several in each direction. Too many people think the only one to be in as a cyclist is the one on the right. Often it is, but not always. General guides for lane choice are speed and direction, with the added criterion of lane width in the case of the cyclist.

The right lane is not the correct choice if you are about to turn left or have just joined the road from a cross street on the left. Nor is it the right choice if the traffic in that lane is perennially being held up by stopped vehicles, or when other traffic in that lane is moving slower than your comfortable speed. On the other hand, it may be your best choice under some of these circumstances namely if

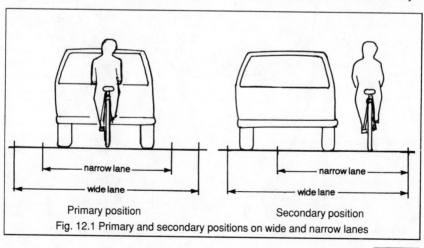

Primary position           Secondary position

Fig. 12.1 Primary and secondary positions on wide and narrow lanes

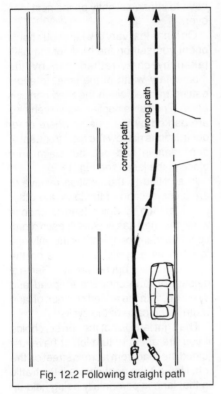

Fig. 12.2 Following straight path

and choose your lane and your position in that lane consciously at all times.

### Thinking Ahead

Riding in traffic is a skill of conscious and constant attention. But the wrong approach is to constantly be prepared for everything. This leads to mental overload and confused or irrational reactions. If you think ahead and use logical reasoning, you are best prepared for the situations and the risks that are relevant at any particular time. This allows you to relax during sections of the trip in which you know the risks to be low. Adjust the things you pay attention to and the intensity of your attention to the relevant situation.

Let's assume a straight road, clear visibility on both sides, no hidden obstructions. There'll not be much to worry about, except from behind, so you relax up front, keep a straight course, listening and looking behind from time to time to make sure nothing is endangering you from that side.

But keep looking ahead and decide whether the situation there changes, so that decisions have to be made. Possible hidden dangers may loom behind

it is so wide that the limiting factors don't interfere with your safe progress. The message is to think about where to be,

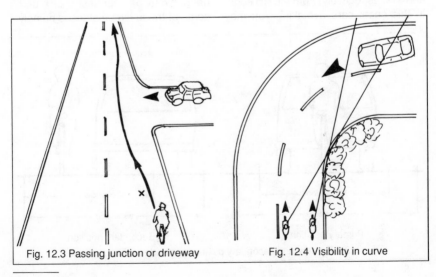

Fig. 12.3 Passing junction or driveway          Fig. 12.4 Visibility in curve

obstructions at the side. Junctions or intersections, lane changes or pedestrian crossings require special actions. Parked vehicles or hazards in the road surface need your attention. Whenever you spot anything,become more alert. Think what may happen in this particular situation — what you may have to do about it, and how that would affect your interaction with other traffic.

Example: bushes by the side of a road in a housing district may hide a child or a dog that will appear quite suddenly (of course clues such as a ball rolling across the road are a dead giveaway that should alert you to the expectation that either the one or the other will be following closely). Think what you can do and what will happen if you do. Decide on your path and pay attention to the situation.

When passing a junction or a driveway, you want to be able to see into that area as soon and as far as possible, and you want to be detected by those emerging from there. You don't want to be caught in a position where you can't escape. All that is avoided by checking behind to make sure the road is clear (in most illustrations, at the point marked X), moving over to the primary position close to the center of the lane (see Fig. 12.3).

The same applies e.g. when approaching a curve to the right with limited visibility: from the middle of the lane — or even from its LH side — you will be able to see around the curve much better (see Fig. 12.4). In all those cases, decide ahead of time where you want to ride, check to make sure there is no traffic immediately behind you, and move over into the proper position in good time, to move back with similar care once you are ready to move to the side of the road.

### Unexpected Obstacles

These are the kind of problems few discussions about traffic ever seem to take notice of. These range from erratic to immobile obstacles. A specific example of the former is what to do around pedestrians. These fellow travelers are totally unpredictable (and should be entitled to that peculiarity). After all, they are not bound to the rules of physics that govern the behavior of wheeled vehicles. Here you will have to keep in mind that you are dealing with something unpredictable.

If you approach a pedestrian from behind, first look back to make sure you can safely move over to keep out of hsi way and do just that. Pedestrians have great respect for motor traffic. However,

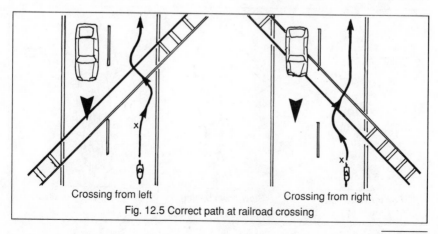

Crossing from left                     Crossing from right
Fig. 12.5 Correct path at railroad crossing

they use their ears to tell them whether anybody is approaching, and your bike doesn't qualify. So if you notice you have not been observed, you may let loose a wild scream at them to make them aware of your presence

An example of the other category of risk is riding across a railway or street-car track running under an angle to the road (see Fig. 12.5). These are real obstacles to bicyclists, whereas they don't qualify as such to anyone else on the road Consequently, motorists following behind will not necessarily understand your behavior as you move over to try and cross them perpendicularly as explained in Chapter 9.

This is one good reason to take your time, looking behind you early enough, signaling if necessary, and moving over only when it is safe to do so. Particularly tricky are those that run from left to right across the road, since you can't time your veering out into the road the way you can when they run the other way.

There are numerous other situations, each requiring a particular logical reaction and each triggering a chain of similar reasoning in your mind. It may be a car parked in a shopping district with somebody in it, so you can figure it may either drive off or a door may swing open. Or it is a driveway or a side road, a pedestrian crossing, or any other potential interference with your movement. In each case, become alert and start thinking what to do well before you get there. Train this kind of selective alertness, perhaps even by making a game of it to gain practice in this method of reasoning, figuring out what to do in traffic, until it has become second nature.

## Hand Signals

Though hand signals are overrated in most forms of presumed safe cycling education, they are important if used correctly. But not in the form of the hands as substitutes for a magic wand, as one can observe only too often not to work. if you stick out your hand, you have not obtained a right of way to do what you have in mind, whether others have seen this signal or not. Mostly, the hand signals, illustrated in Fig. 12.6 serve two functions, namely as a negotiating tool and as a form of politeness. Signals need not be given continuously: about one second at a time at 5 to 10 second intervals, is quite adequate to be detected.

For the beginning cyclist, it's best to think only of the latter function. To turn right stretch out the right hand (for the

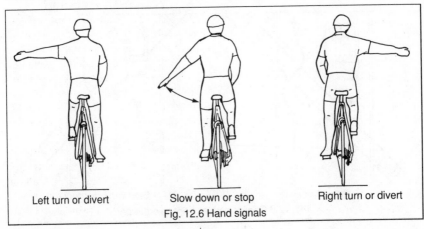

Left turn or divert            Slow down or stop            Right turn or divert
Fig. 12.6 Hand signals

cyclist, this is preferable to the motorist's signal made by pointing the left hand up) This in effect tells drivers, cyclists or pedestrians who would cut across your path if you were goign straight, 'Don't worry about me, I'll be out of your way.' Or wave the left hand up and down to indicate to those following you that you will be stopping, meaning they can overtake you (but be smart enough to move over to the right as you stop).

The left turning signal, made by stretching out the left hand, has its dangers. To turn left, you usually have to cross the path of others, both from behind and from in front. Doing that is only safe when you have first looked behind you to verify there is no other vehicle following so closely behind as to be affected by your move — and then there is nobody to signal to.

Now you are safe to proceed to the center of the road, but you still have to cross the path of approaching vehicles, who have the right of way and don't need

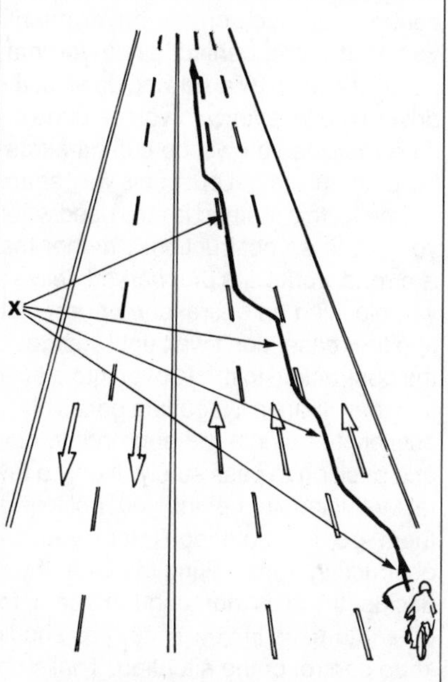

Fig. 12.7 Staggered lane changing

your hand signal to confuse them. The only people to whom you may politely indicate your intention to turn off to the left may be pedestrians on the other side of the intersection, whom you can tell this way that you won't be cutting across their path.

## Negotiating Techniques

Movement along your lane is easy and riskless enough, as long as you ride predictably and don't deviate from your position in the lane. But whenever you have to move sideways, whether that is to turn off, to stop, to overtake another vehicle or to pass an obstacle, you may have to negotiate your way over, because you are likely to encroach upon the paths of other road users.

In its simplest, submissive or passive form, negotiating amounts to checking behind to make sure the road is clear for you to move over. Look back well before you get to the point where you have to move over or turn off, and repeat the process until you have established a safe time to move. When the distance to the next vehicle behind you is so great in relation to its speed that you are not at risk, move over to the other side of your lane, repeating the process for other lanes if there are several in your direction, until you have arrived in the middle of the road (see Fig. 12.7).

Once you are near the middle of the road, you may have to start negotiating for a chance to cross the path of the traffic in the opposite direction. If necessary, stop the bike in a low enough gear to start off and wait for a gap in the approaching traffic before you move over, swinging into your correct path, depending where you are going.

If you are turning left, that correct path is not one monstrous big swing to the RH side of the crossing road, but instead a relatively short swing to the middle of the leftmost traffic lane (assuming it has several lanes in that direction). To get back to the primary position in the middle of the RH lane of the crossing road, or the secondary one on the RH side of that same lane, you start negotiating all over again, looking behind to find a safe time to move over in half-lane steps until you are in your final position.

That's defensive negotiation. It's the method that should be used by those who are not 100% sure of themselves yet. The advanced form of negotiation is a more two-sided affair. Don't try it until you are confident about both your motor skills on the bike and your traffic sense as it applies to coordinating your movements to those of other road users.

### Advanced Negotiating

In advanced, or interactive negotiation, you look the other fellow in the eye. See, he's looking back at you — he knows what you have in mind, especially if you move up from the exclusively polite to the negotiating use of the hand signal, which is OK once you have reached this point. Now your chances to be let in don't only depend on the size of the gap and the initial speed of the other vehicle: your negotiating efforts influence the opponent's behavior. Not everybody's: some of those rats will keep going as fast as ever and make no bones about it. But you only need one to take action — providing you have developed the ability to judge the way he behaves correctly. If you get the chance, acknowledge the friendly gesture with a nod or a smile, looking the driver right in the face again.

Don't expect him to get out of the car and shout, "OK, bicyclist, you can come in ahead of me now." Instead, you will be the one who has to judge from the slight change in motor noise, or even from the look on the driver's face, whether it will be safe to go. The first time you try this, you will perhaps miss

as many chance as you get. But sooner or later, you will get the hang of it and within a week you'll be negotiating as though you've done it all your life. Actually, chances are you have: in many other aspects of life we use similar techniques, even though the physical risk of misjudgment is not usually as acute as it is when cycling in traffic.

This technique is not only used when moving over for a left turn or a lane change. The same applies when you enter from a side street at a stop sign or from a driveway. In that case you must also make sure your bike is in the proper (low) gear and is positioned so that you can move right into place when the opportunity arrives.

In high-density, high-speed traffic, such as where accelerating lanes, or slip roads, lead on or off expressways, or where unique direction lanes and free-flow lanes must be entered or crossed to get to your right path, the same negotiating techniques are used. In some of these cases, you should concentrate as much on the driver next to you as the one behind, since you may as well be let in by a slowing down of the driver who is level with you — certainly if he realizes you will be cutting across his path only to get out of his way again.

Finally, this method is also used when you get to an obstruction, whether that is a road works site or a parked delivery van blocking an entire lane or part of it. In either case, don't wait until you get to the obstruction to move over into a position that clears it. Negotiate passively or actively to get into the appropriate lane and position to pass safely. If only a few fast vehicles are behind you, politely let them go first, but don't feel you are obstructing traffic taking the lane. If you decide there is not enough room for others to pass in your lane, *you* should keep control of the situation. That's not lane hogging but safe cycling practice.

# 13. Dealing with Specific Traffic Situations

In this chapter, you will get the opportunity to use the basic skills that were explained in Chapter 12. Your newly gained understanding of the basic principles used will make it easier to follow and apply these methods in concrete situations, some of which may seem difficult or irrational to the beginning cyclist. Whatever you do, continue to think ahead. Decide on a safe course of action, and consider the alternatives open to you if the situation changes well ahead of the relevant location.

I generally refer to *vehicles* or *traffic*, rather than to *cars*. That's because few of these situations are restricted to motor vehicles only. In fact, the only serious bicycle accident I've had myself was when a slower cyclist, whom I was overtaking, turned left unexpectedly in front of me.

Few really experienced cyclists fear traffic — or many other hazards of cycling for that matter. Yet many a more recent convert to the sport is filled with fear most of his cycling life. Wait five years and 20,000 miles, whichever comes last, and he will have licked the problem too. But he may have died long before that — if not in an accident, then perhaps of fear. There are better ways of learning such relatively complex skills as are required for safe cycling in heavy traffic than by trial and error. It's better to learn from the experience of others. That's what this chapter will allow you to do: you'll learn from my mistakes, rather than having to make your own.

When deciding which of the many different traffic situations to cover, I shall be using three criteria:

* Situations that are feared most by the majority of cyclists;

* Situations that most frequently lead to accidents;

* Accidents that most frequently lead to serious injuries.

### Stabbed in the Back?

What seems to be prevalent on nearly every beginning cyclist's mind, being most universally feared, is the chance of being hit while overtaken by a faster moving vehicle. It does not rate very high at all as a frequent cause of accidents (less than one percent of all reported accidents are of this type), but when it does happen, it tends to be serious: a high percentage of fatal accidents on rural roads (not on urban roads) are of this type. That's probably

Urban cycling amidst dense traffic. Here shown in London, a city where 15 years ago hardly anybody cycled at all. It requires some special skills but is not hard to learn and not inherently unsafe.

mainly due to the unexpectedness of such accidents, which does not allow any averting action on the cyclists' part.

Such accidents of this type as do happen turn out to be mostly mislabelled. Far from the cyclist following his straight course while some vindictive motorist sweeps him down from behind, the overwhelming majority are the result of the cyclist's diverting from his straight and predictable course without taking concern for those following closely behind.

Keep a good distance from the RH curb, determine your course around obstacles in and along the road well in advance, and check behind you to make sure you can move over to the left without infringing on the course of those following behind. Don't move out when the coast is not clear: wait until there is a suitable gap in the traffic. The same goes if you want to reach some destination on the LH side of the road or to move over to a traffic lane further left, either to turn left or to go straight where the other traffic in your lane is turning right.

However, some of these accidents don't involve the actual purposeful diversion on the part of the bicyclist. He may have diverted, but not intentionally. Be particularly on your guard for this kind of accident on narrow rural roads, especially under one of the following circumstances:

*   When there is relatively dense traffic coming the other way;

*   When a low sun or other visibility factors make it likely you may not be noticed in time by the drivers of following vehicles.

The latter case is the more difficult to deal with, because you can't very well be checking behind you and getting ready to throw yourself in the ditch continuously. Just look when there is a sound that indicates someone following, especially if no slowing of the motor noise indicates the driver is reacting to your presence. Good lighting by night and perhaps particularly brightly colored clothing by day may minimize the risk.

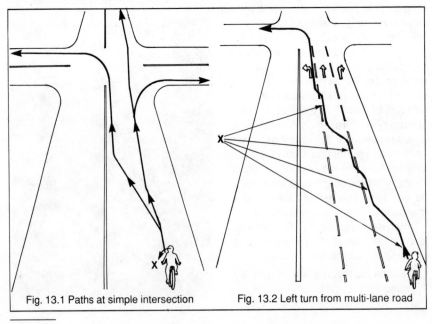

Fig. 13.1 Paths at simple intersection          Fig. 13.2 Left turn from multi-lane road

## Intersections

First I shall describe the conplex of the intersection as a whole. Curiously, most people fear only one kind of movement, namely the left turn. In fact, more accidents happen to those going straight than turning left, exactly because they don't realize there may be a problem when going straight. I'd go even further: most left-turn accidents are really mislabelled straight through collisions, since the cyclist wanting to turn left tried to do that by going straight to the other side of the intersection, then turned the bike 90 degrees to go straight across the other leg. That's the worst way of doing it. Let's look at the whole complex.

Intersections are dangerous places because different vehicles cut across one another's path. You can make any maneuver there safer by minimizing this path-crossing. That's done by selecting your correct path early — well before you get to the intersection. The general concept as it applies to a simple intersection is illustrated in Fig. 13.1. With at least 50 m (150 ft) to go before the inter-

section — more if the traffic is dense and fast — think where you want to be to minimize crossing others' paths once you get there: left to turn left, in the middle to go straight and nearer the RH side or in the middle to turn right. The latter may come as a surprise to some — why not hug the curb there if you turn right anyway. That is done to discourage others from overtaking you in the curve, squeezing you off the road.

Note the crosses in the illustration: those are the locations where you have to look behind, checking to make sure the coast is clear — and don't move over until it is, even if it means you have to repeat it a number of times. A slightly different situation occurs when there is not a full intersection but a junction — either a T-junction or a side street to one side. The guiding principles still apply: think well ahead, select the correct path and don't move over until it is safe to do so. We'll now take the various maneuvers one at a time.

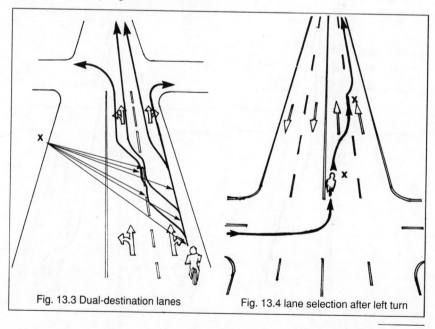

Fig. 13.3 Dual-destination lanes    Fig. 13.4 lane selection after left turn

## Left turn

Turning left from any busy road, especially if other traffic travels fast, is a novice cyclist's nightmare. And out of fear for this situation, thousands of cyclists each year get involved in just this kind of accident. In their obsessive fear they do exactly what makes this maneuver dangerous: stay glued to the RH side of the road and then suddenly turn off at the last moment. To turn left, you first have to be near the center of the road, or — in the case of a multi-lane road — in a lane designated for turning left.

Sounds reasonable enough, but how do you get there? Not the way most of the accident victims do, namely after hugging the RH side of the road up to the last second. In essentially every non-freeway situation, there are quite adequate gaps between vehicles in each lane to allow traversing one lane at a time (see Fig. 13.2). I have demonstrated this by taking quite young children on very heavily (and quite fast) trafficked roads and performing left turns. It can be done safely once you know how to go about it.

Start well ahead of the intersection or junction; traverse from your initial position to the LH side of your lane, than to the RH side of the next lane — one lane at a time; each time look behind you before you leave your position, waiting for an adequate gap in the faster traffic following in that lane. If you miss the turn (it sometimes happens to the best of us), stay in the lane you are and either negotiate your way over in time for the next turn or similarly find your way back to the RH side.

Often certain lanes are destined for two ultimate directions, e.g. left turn and straight ahead (see Fig. 13.3). A frequent cause of accidents in this situation is the cyclist's insistence to hug the RH side of whatever lane he is in. Don't get caught this way to the right of straight through traffic if you're turning left. Normally, take the primary position near the middle of the lane; if you've made sure all the traffic following in that same lane will be going straight, you take the LH

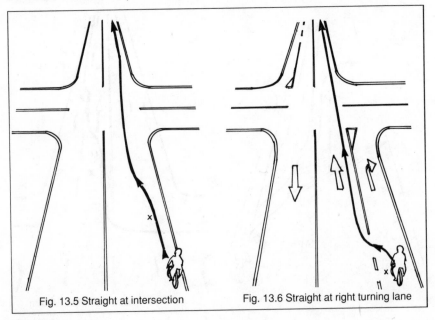

Fig. 13.5 Straight at intersection          Fig. 13.6 Straight at right turning lane

side of the lane. This allows them to pass to your right, assuming adequate lane width. But be just as much on your guard not to be caught to the left of faster left-turning vehicles.

Depending on the traffic and the number of lanes in the road into which you turn, you should usually enter the primary position of the inside lane, or whichever lane corresponds most closely to your initial position (see Flg. 13.4). Once you are going straight in the new road, start moving over to your eventual riding position in your chosen lane. Follow the staggered procedure described above if necessary, and always check behind you before you leave your current path.

### Straight ahead

Going straight at a junction or intersection does not rate very high on the average cyclist's list of most dreaded maneuvers. Yet it's probably about the most accident-prone situation. As with the left turn, it's a matter of choosing the correct path: if you want to go straight, don't be caught to the right of faster traffic turning right — nor to the left of others turning left (see Fig. 13.5).

When going straight at major road junctions with slip roads or separate left-turning lanes, avoid getting into those special right-turn 'channels' in good time (see Fig. 13.6). Use the same technique described above: look ahead to make sure where you want to go, check behind, waiting for a gap in following traffic, and move over to the appropriate side of the lane, until you have reached your proper position in the correct traffic lane. In a multi-destination lane, stay in the middle, unless you can be sure those behind you will all be turning off, in which case you can allow them to overtake you on the appropriate side, providing the lane is wide enough.

### Roundabouts

These are the curious gyratories for circular traffic at intersections, so popular in Great Britain, but also found elsewhere. Roundabouts form a special case of junction complication, feared by many cyclists. Yet the very concept of the roundabout is one of minimizing risks by providing a system in which one only has to deal with traffic from one direction. Once more, what gets cyclists into trouble is primarily their reluctance

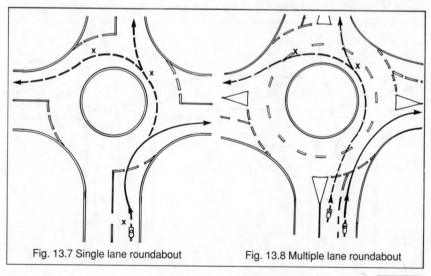

Fig. 13.7 Single lane roundabout          Fig. 13.8 Multiple lane roundabout

to get away from the RH edge of the road. Within the roundabout, as well as at its approaches, the extreme right is only for those intending to take the next exit. Thus, the fearful curb-hugging cyclist puts himself in a position to be cut off by faster drivers who do want to turn off.

Follow one of the two courses illustrated in Fig. 13.7 and 13.8 for single and multiple lane systems, respectively. In the single lane roundabout, keep close to the middle of the lane, except in the last segment before exiting. In a multi-lane roundabout, the actual choice of lane depends on the volume and prevalent destination of the other traffic. Just don't get too far over to the right (the 'outside') if you have to stay on the roundabout, nor too far over to the left (the 'inside') just before turning off.

### Through Traffic Turning Off

Especially in older road systems, the through traffic — the main road so to speek — does not always continue straight at cross-roads and junctions. Fig. 13.9 illustrates a typical situation where the direction of the priority traffic turns off to the right. As a cyclist, it is no problem if you want to follow the same route as the rest of the traffic: you turn right from the primary position as though you were going straight.

But what to do if you have to go straight across, or even turn left, though everybody else goes to the right? In effect, you have to do what you would have to do to turn off to the left, which you are indeed doing — relative to the main traffic direction. Well before the junction, start negotiating to move over to the center of the road. If necessary, slow down or even stop in the center, just before the middle of the curve. Wait there until a gap appears in the opposing traffic and go when it is safe to do so, cutting the shortest possible path across to your destination lane, entering it near the LH side. Finally negotiate your way over to the primary or the secondary riding position in the appropriate lane.

### One-Way Systems

Ride on one-way roads as though they are the RH side of a two-way road, and you will be reasonably safe and confident. The greatest danger of one-way systems is not riding along them, but crossing them. You are subconsciously trained to expect traffic coming from the left before you run into traffic coming

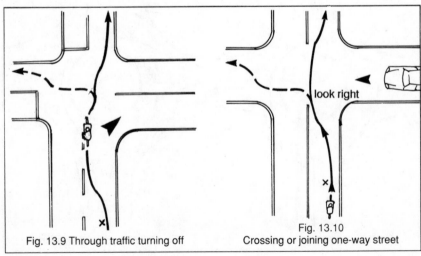

Fig. 13.9 Through traffic turning off

Fig. 13.10
Crossing or joining one-way street

from the right. When crossing a one-way road coming from the right, there will be nothing coming from the other side, and in your excitement about this rare treat you may forget to worry about vehicles crossing your path from the right — riding what seems like the wrong side of the road (see Fig. 13.10).

Turning into and out of one-way roads also takes some special precautions. It's a matter of finding the right position in the lane. Once more, it helps if you think of the one way road as just one half of a normal road. Often traffic on one-way systems travels faster than it does on other streets, so be particularly on guard to select your position in the lane early and move over decisively when it is safe to do so.

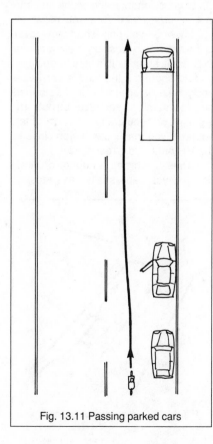

Fig. 13.11 Passing parked cars

## Traffic Dodging

There is one traffic situation which seems to defy rational cycling techniques: urban rush hour traffic. For the cars, it's bumper-to-bumper. For cyclists and motorcyclists it's a challenge. It is probably exactly this situation that has led to the phenomenal increase of popularity of these modes of transport in many major cities where cyclists and motorcyclists were at best a *quantité négligeable* up to about 10 years ago.

What these two-wheeled wizards do is usually illegal, and generally dangerous, but it does seem to make sense: they take advantage of the limited width of their vehicles, darting in and out, overtaking on either side.

Being a little more cautious than most, I usually don't partake in this. I have witnessed too many near-misses and some real hits, usually resulting when a right-overtaking cyclist runs into the RH side of a car as it is pulling up or turning right next to or just ahead of him. Speeds being low, such accidents are rarely very serious. Just the same, I rather wait behind a slowly crawling line of cars than risking my life passing it.

But I shall not deny that it is done with great gains in time and tolerable risk by many. Who am I to tell you it's dangerous? Just keep in mind that those cars are occupied by people who may have other things on their minds than perennially considering some crazy cyclist will come shooting out of every gap. You can probably do it if you think about the impact of your actions, realizing how you would act if you were in one of the cars you're overtaking ever which way. It *is* a challenge.

In this same densely trafficked urban environment, many cyclists feel a particularly strong urge to move over as close to the curb as possible. However, that curb lane is frequently interrupted, i.e. with parked cars and stopping busses or taxis. Just about the worst thing you can do is weave around obstacles like that. Indeed, the cause of many urban accidents is exactly the unpredictability of the cyclist's entering, leaving and reentering the regular traffic stream wherever such obstacles interrupt the curb lane.

Instead, choose a straight course, far enough to the left of any obstacles to stay out of their way. That means far enough even when car doors are suddenly opened or when pedestrians just as suddenly step off the sidewalk (see Fig. 13.11). Depending on the width of the road, you may be able to find your own track between parked vehicles and moving ones, at other times you may have to ride near the center of the lane.

Generally, there is enough road width to allow faster vehicles to pass you on your left. But even if there isn't, don't fear you're holding up traffic. In more than thirty years of following this technique, I do not remember a traffic jam ever being caused by the delay my presence might have caused. Of course, when the curbside is clear over a longer distance and several vehicles are eager to overtake, you can judiciously get out of their way temporarily, reclaiming your path near the middle of the lane when they

have overtaken you. Just don't forget to look behind you and don't leave your straight course unless you've established that it is safe to do so.

## Stopping in Traffic

There are three situations where you will have to stop in traffic:

*   at a traffic light or a stop sign;

*   in straight-through traffic, if the vehicles in front of you are stopped;

*   at intersections, waiting for a gap in the crossing traffic that is big enough to allow you through safely.

When stopping at a traffic light or a stop sign, generally do so near the middle of the lane. You don't want to have some clown pass you there and squeeze you out of your rightful place as the first one in line. Just make sure you move off quickly when you can. Then move over to the secondary position to allow others to pass as soon as it is safe to do so — and no sooner. If the lane is very wide and you know for sure the traffic stopped next to you will not squeeze you out turning right, or if you are turning right or left yourself, you may instead stop close to the RH or LH side, respectively.

If a line of vehicles is stopped at a traffic light, you can usually pass most of

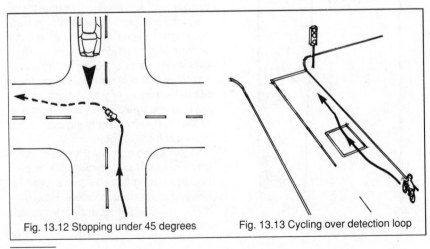

Fig. 13.12 Stopping under 45 degrees          Fig. 13.13 Cycling over detection loop

them — preferably to their left, but if enough width is available, that may be done very carefully on the right. It will be best to take your place just behind the first car — and move off without holding up the one following. Always make sure you are clearly visible to the driver behind you, and get out of his way so he may overtake once it is safe to do so. After all, you just squeezed in front of him and it's live and let live in bicycle commuting.

When stopped in traffic that has just stalled, you are usually best advised to do just like the others, without dodging between lines of stalled traffic: stop in the middle of your lane. However, if the delay appears to be unreasonably long, use the traffic dodging technique described above to pass these stalled

vehicles. The justification for this behavior is twofold:

**1.** Physically, traffic is stalled only because the width of those vehicles is such that they can't pass, whereas your bike is narrow enough to get by.

**2.** Morally, bicyclists are not the cause of the problem but the solution: there'd be no jam if the others were riding bikes too.

When stopped at an intersection to turn left, you will want to make yourself both clearly visible to others and yet minimize the chances of being hit on account of your visible width relative to the available road width. Do that by turning the bike under about 45 degrees, as shown in Fig. 13.12. It also sets you up in a position to start off most conveniently.

Looks more idyllic than it turns out to be. Such cycling facilities, shown here in the Dutch town of Tilburg, don't contribute anything to the cyclist's safety — in fact, they expose him to some special risks, due to the unpredictability of the other users. When fewer cyclists use them, additional dangers would be due to the unusual interaction with crossing traffic

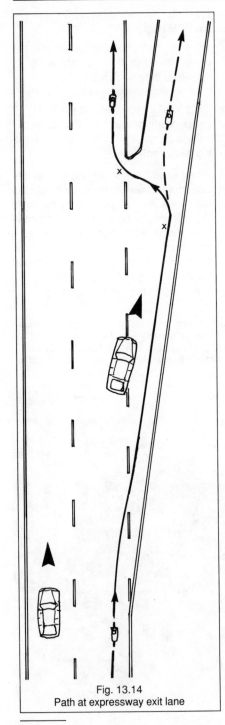

Fig. 13.14
Path at expressway exit lane

### Traffic Detectors

Many traffic lights are activated by means of induction loops. These are coils of electric wire buried under the road surface in which the passing of a mass of metal generates an electric signal that controls the traffic light's switching program. Their outline is usually marked by means of a white border painted on the road surface. All cars have enough metal on them to be detected by any of these contraptions. Consequently, traffic lights controlled by a detection loop will go green eventually after a car has crossed the loop. But some are not sensitive enough to respond to the bike's little mass of metal. At low-traffic times, you may not be willing to wait for the next car to come along (I have on one occasion clocked 17 minutes waiting time if a cyclist would have been dumb enough to do so).

Be suspicious when the painted outline is short: whereas the long rectangular loops are always sensitive enough to detect cyclists, many of the short ones are not. Ride over any loop in the location marked (see Fig. 13.13), about 60 cm (2 ft) to the inside from one of the sides. If it obviously doesn't react — more than a minute waiting time is unreasonable — start checking on the cross traffic and eventually move across the intersection when it is safe to do so.

### Expressway Cycling

Under this concept, I shall cover some of the techniques necessary to handle the rather inhibiting situations typical for roads built for high volumes and elevated speeds. Contrary to popular belief, these roads are not inherently unsafe for cycling, though they are so for incompetent cyclists.

Lane holding and turning practices on these roads are the same as apply on other multi-lane roads. The only difference is that these roads have very few crossings and side streets (making them inherently both faster and safer for cyclists as much as for others). Besides, what traffic is let on and off from and to crossing or joining roads is usually guided along slip roads, i.e. acceleration and deceleration lanes. The cyclist is confronted with the question where he should be riding, both when continuing straight along the main road and when joining it or turning off.

When riding along such a road, you will more frequently find it to your advantage to adhere to the secondary position close to the RH side of the RH lane. Since the other traffic is faster and denser than it is on most other roads, and since the lanes are typically wide, this will be your safest and most convenient position.

To continue straight at a right turning lane, you may feel safer to join the use that lane until it separates from the raod and then negotiate your way back to your oritinal position (see Fig. 12.14). If speed and density are moderate, just keep to the primary position and ignore the decelartion lane. Either mehtod prevents others from cutting across your path to reach the deceleration lane.

When turning off from an expressway, seek out the deceleration lane as early as you can, and move to its RH side. This prevents confrontations with other and faster vehicles turning off after you who might otherwise cut across your path.

When continuing straight at a feeder lane entering from the right (Fig. 13.15), it is often reasonable to get out of the traffic coming on from the right. Do that by checking the situation in that lane and cutting across to its RH side, to follow that lane back onto the main road. This is really the only situation in which it is safer for a bicyclist to follow a different course than what would be appropriate for a motor vehidle.

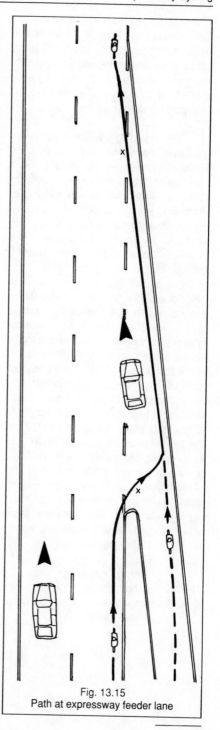

Fig. 13.15
Path at expressway feeder lane

To enter an expressway from a feeder lane, stay in the middle or on the RH side as long as possible, to avoid being cut off by other drivers behind you overtaking you on your right. Wait until an adequate gap appears in the traffic on the expressway and move into place.

### Overtaking and Passing

You overtake slower vehicles or pass fixed obstacles — be they parked vehicles or road works — essentially on their left. What most cyclists will have to learn and practice though, is to move into position to do so *early*. Don't wait until you get there, but move over like you would for a left turn, after checking behind you for a gap in the traffic.

If the road is too narrow for traffic in both directions simultaneously, especially at a road works site, a shuttle lane is usually in effect. This situation is most typically controlled by means of a traffic light or a flag man. But it may be less formal if the density of the traffic does not justify it, especially at such obstructions as a narrow bridge. In either case, remember that you have as much right to the road as the person in a car. If the road is clear when you get there, just keep going, preferably fast. If you have to stop, move into position at the head of the line. If only a few cars are waiting stay in the rear or let them go first. Otherwise, just take your place and only allow others to pass you in locations where *you* decide it is safe to do so.

### Being Overtaken

The denser the traffic and the higher its speed in comparison to yours, the more frequently you will be overtaken by other road users. As suggested before, it is smarter to stay in control yourself. Do that by normally riding in the primary position near the middle of the lane, especially if the road (or the particular lane in which you are) is too narrow for continuous side-by-side travel of bikes and cars.

When the lane is narrow and another lane in the same direction is available for overtaking — and not occupied by a dense stream of vehicles — stay where you are. This forces the overtaking motorist to pass you in that overtaking lane, which is safer for everybody concerned and doesn't slow down anybody.

If no overtaking lane is free and you notice someone wants to overtake you, look back and acknowledge his presence by looking him in the face. Then either move over to the secondary position further to the right (if you are sure it is safe for you to do so right away), or stay where you are until you have reached a point where you decide that it *is* safe to be overtaken.

Also take traffic coming the other way into consideration in this kind of situation. Don't encourage overtaking if that might put the motorists overtaking you in conflict with those coming towards you. Not only for *their* safety, but also for your own and that of other road users: when the two motorists notice they are in one another's way, one or the other may finish up running you or someone else off the road. The competent cyclist stays in control of the situation through the correct choice of his or her position in the road.

# 14. Practical Aspects of Bicycle Commuting

In this chapter we shall look at some of the everyday considerations that influence the commuting cyclist's routine. In fact, as in the rest of the book, we'll look just a little beyond bicycle commuting and consider all forms of utility cycling. The most important aspects can probably be wrapped up with the formula *extending the bicycle's utility*.

What limits it — at least in the eyes of most people — is a number of different restrictions they perceive. Specifically, the bicycle's use is often considered hampered by inadequacies in the following areas:

* carrying capacity
* traveling speed
* traveling range
* nighttime use
* bad weather use
* dress codes
* parking

All of these limitations are merely perceived. In different parts of the world, different people habitually overcome one or more of these, and it is not impossible to overcome all of them compounded. We'll take them one at a time.

## Carrying Capacity

Touring cyclists regularly carry a full set of camping equipment, tools, food and clothing, weighing up to 25 kg (55 lbs)

Cycling photographer Ben Swets, demonstrating how practical the bicycle can be. He arrives at the job site or the editing studion with all he needs loaded on the bike. The front container with video casettes lifts off the rack and can be carried straight into the building.

on the bike. That's a lot of gear, outweighing the typical small household grocery shopping load — or for that matter any load that is typically carried in a car. Some people take the car to buy a package of cigarettes two blocks away. Rather ironic to hear those same folks put down the bike as having inadequate carrying capacity. Even if it doesn't carry a wardrobe or a refrigerator (though I have seen some extraordinary examples of bicycle transportation of this kind using bicycle trailers), most cars are not suitable for those loads either, and generally such items are delivered to the house.

The same weight and volume that can be carried on a camping trip — and more — can easily be transported over shorter distances on urban trips. Mount sturdy racks front and rear and invest in a couple of webbing straps with buckles to attach almost any load to the bike. You don't need to be carrying lots of heavy gear on the bike all the time, but don't feel inhibited: it can be done, and it makes sense to equip the bike to do it when needed.

Individual cyclists have come up with clever solutions. Such as the large container Los Angeles photographer Ben Smets uses to carry his materials, or the

piece of plastic drain pipe that can be used to carry long, relatively narrow upright items, ranging from a roll of drawings or a projection screen to a curtain rail. Or take small scale publisher Anne Modersohn, who designed the clever support to carry squarish packages of almost any size. Shown in Fig. 14.1, it is cut from a plastic container and serves as well to hold a shopping bag as it does to carry a 36 lbs box full of books. I'm not telling you to copy those designs, but I am suggesting you should consider such solutions if you ever have a similar need, or be inspired by the kind of thinking that went into their design to solve your particular carrying problems.

### Traveling Speed

Some cyclists are slow, but not all cycling necessarily *has* to be slow. Nor can it be said that all motoring is necessarily fast — not to mention public transportation, which is often dismally slow if you include waiting time and the trips to and from stops or stations. Take a look at Fig. 14.2 to see just how well bicycling compares with other forms of transportation in urban areas. And those are figures that apply to the average, slow, cyclist. You can do better than that if you are in a hurry. Also consider the other aspect: if you like cycling anyway, then it may be hard to get an hour's cycling in every day in addition to your regular day's activities. Choosing to commute by bike, two half hour commuting trips (or any number of minor utility rides) soon add up to quite a respectable cycling mileage.

Cycling seems to come natural to most people at a speed of about 10 mph (16 km/h), accounting for stops in city traffic. On an open road, that speed increases to about 13 mph (20 km/h). A trained cyclist can ride at about 20 mph (32 km/h) for about an hour without exhaustion. However, the average drops

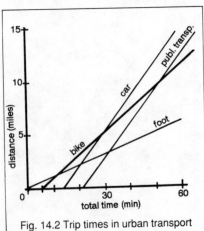

Fig. 14.2 Trip times in urban transport

off dramatically when frequent stops in urban traffic make it hard to push the average beyond 13 mph (20 km/h). But even that is not a bad speed, when you consider the distances most people have to cover. Often half an hour's cycling gets you beyond the limits of most cities from the downtown area. And the rest of the way — if you have to travel further — can be done at the much better speed. No, the bike is not inherently too slow for most commuting and other utility uses.

### Traveling Range

Very much the same as was said about speed can be said about range: In relation to most trips, the bicycle is a sensible means of transport. Just do it selectively: take the car or get a ride if the distances are such that on the bike they would exceed the available time. I know of cyclists who regularly commute 20 miles each way, while others think their 2-mile trip is too long to handle on the bike. It's all in the way you feel about cycling.

Even if you live 40 miles from your job, there are opportunities to use the bike. Join with others in a car pool and meet them at some point along the route. Or use public transportation for part of your journey, either leaving the bike at a safe place or dismantling it to carry on board. Where carrying a bike is not allowed, a simple bag to hide it, as shown in Fig. 14.3, will do the trick for a normal bike. Note that the carrying strap attaches to the frame, rather than to the bag.

Obviously, light folding bikes are a nice solution for mixed transport. Though new designs of this kind turn up on a regular basis, only few are of the quality that makes them even remotely as pleasant and safe to ride as most derailleur bikes are. Honorable mentions should go to the Bickerton and the Moulton, though the latter is both extremely expensive and relatively bulky to transport. The relatively widely distributed DaHon at least folds up compactly, though the cycling comfort is marginal at best, especially for taller riders.

### Cycling in Bad Weather

I shall never forget my first group ride in the US. After having lived and cycled most of my life in such rainy regions as Britain and Holland, I had made arrangements with some colleagues in California for a Sunday bike tour. At seven in the morning the phone rang: "There's a 20% chance of rain, so we'll

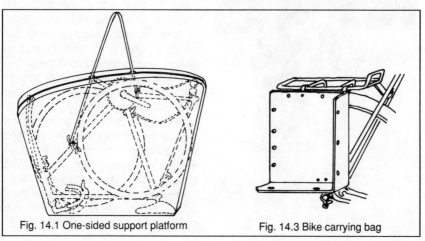

Fig. 14.1 One-sided support platform                    Fig. 14.3 Bike carrying bag

have to call off the ride," I was informed. That seemed a curious attitude and I went on the ride anyway, together with two other 'hardy' cyclists. We had a wonderful day. It didn't rain — after all with 80%, the odds were in our favor.

But even if it had rained, we would have had a pretty good ride: though rain may distract from the pleasure of cycling, it is not usually so serious that it becomes punishment. And the same can be said for all kinds of other weather problems, ranging from snow to wind and from excessive heat to frost.

Consider that in any part of the world cyclists have got to accept what seems normal. In British Columbia or the Pacific Northwest it rains. Everybody knows it and so you don't stop cycling if it does. You dress for it or you ignore it, but you wouldn't lose a night's sleep worrying about it. The same can be said for the cold in other parts of the world: if

Don't give up bicycle commuting when it gets cold. Just dress warmer and continue using the bike.

it often freezes or snows, you just learn to ride when it is that way. At the other extreme, I don't go for heat too much, but folks in much of the Midwest or the South, where it does get hot, seem to think nothing of riding their bikes at 100 degrees F (38 degrees C).

The message is simple: keep in mind what can be done — and enjoyed — in other parts of the world, and start doing it yourself. Buy the clothing that keeps you reasonably dry and warm (or cool), equip the bike with fenders to keep the spray off in the rain, with pedal covers to protect your feet in the cold. Not necessarily all the time, but install and wear whatever seems appropriate for the least favorable conditions that can be expected at any particular time. Refer to chapters 5 and 6 for a review of the available gear for these purposes.

### Cycling in the Dark

Yes, you can cycle at night. The same applies here as was said with respect to inclement weather. In my native Holland and in the North of England, where I spent a good part of my early cycling days, it gets dark pretty early and light pretty late in winter. That makes for lots of hours of darkness and some people would say lots of time unsuitable for cycling. Rubbish: with decent bike lights, you can cycle quite well in the dark. I have mentioned the equipment requirements in Chapter 5, and there is not much more to know about the subject than how to keep them in working order.

In addition to lights and reflectors, you may consider increasing your conspicuity by wearing highly visible clothing. But don't think screaming orange or ugly green will do the trick. What you need at night is very light clothing. White is best, followed by bright yellow — and it only works while someone elses headlight is aimed at you. There are some specially treated materials on the market for cycling wear that are treated with a reflective coating. Available in a neutral gray, these garmente are almost as visible in the beam of an approaching car as though you were wearing a lilly white outfit.

I've experienced a few near misses at night though — both with pedestrians and with (unlit) cyclists. One good reason to avoid like the plague using anything other than regular roads at night. No bike paths, no off-road shortcuts, no sidewalks. You will have to train yourself for night cycling, because it does take some getting used to. Keep in mind that you can't be seen except by your lights and (by those following behind) your rear reflector. But hand signals — not even very useful by day — will remain totally invisible to others. Also remember that spoke reflectors (or reflective tire sidewalls) do not 'ligth up' to those who are coming out of a side street, because their lights are not aimed at them at the time you and the other driver should take action about one another.

### Dress Codes

Yes, you can cycle in civil clothes, even though special cycling dress is generally more comfortable and indeed often more effective for traveling longer distances at elevated speeds. But I can also reveal that my father commuted by bike for thirty years before he realized there was such a thing as special bike dress — and then only because his son had taken up bike racing. A five mile ride is nothing unusual in normal dress, certainly if you keep the guidelines for civil dress that I gave in Chapter 6 in mind.

However, it is entirely possible to carry out an effective transformation between stopping the bike and going inside. I perform this act whenever I go to the theater or the symphony, a restaurant or any official place of business: button up my

shirt, pull up my tie, change my sneakers for dress shoes, dab my face with a hand towel (and if necessary some water from my water bottle), and comb my hair. Takes two minutes at the most and works wonders for your public image — if that should be any concern to you.

The accessories needed for this Cinderella act are easily carried on the bike or in a bag. To my mind, they should not be missing from any bike commuter's packing list: comb, towel, deodorant, water bottle. And the spare pair of shoes may be superfluous if you select respectable looking light footwear with a thin but rigid leather sole in the first place.

### Parking the Bike

Finally, there is the aspect to consider of what to do with the bike while you are out doing your thing. This includes both the consideration of bike theft and safety of the bike and its equipment. The former you have to just keep in mind at all times when leaving the bike, asking yourself whether this is a place where a bike thief or one who gets his kicks vandalizing bikes would feel at ease or not. The presence of plenty of pedestrians typically discourages those characters. Don't leave the bike tucked away in a hidden corner, because though nobody

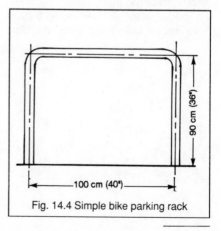

Fig. 14.4 Simple bike parking rack

Another practical solution of the carrying problem. Independent book publisher Anne Modersohn developed this one-sided platform that allows carrying anything big and rectangular. It's the way she carried her computer home and the way she takes her books to the post office.

else will notice it, your typical bike pilferer no doubt will, feeling quite uninhibited to go about his work.

Specific bicycle parking facilities have been provided in many places. Most are no good whatsoever. I remember $ 2000 bike racks being installed on San Francisco's Market Street that remained empty, because they could hold no more than the front wheel of a size incompatible with most bikes on the street: neither narrow racing tires nor fat mountain bike rubbers would fit. And even if it did, the wheel was likely to be bent and the rest of the bike stolen.

The best simple bike rack is the one illustrated in Fig. 14.4. Yes, that's no more than a short piece of simple railing as you will find in many places to keep pedestrians at bay (except that ideally it is only three feet long and placed in the middle of the sidewalk, so bikes can be placed at both sides. Short of somebody installing those things specially for bike parking, find yourself a piece of fence and lock the bike up to it. If you have to lock the bike to a tree or a post, place it so that it does not roll backward, by turning the crank back to the point where the pedal on the side of the post is in top and rests against it.

Even for short stops at offices, shops and the like, always lock the bike firmly to something. Both the large U-locks and a very strong cable lock may be suitable — though the latter only in low-risk areas: don't leave a bike locked with anything less than a U-lock in the dark or in any area with minimal pedestrian traffic even during the day. To take the accessories with you, use an easily removable (and easily carried) bag that is normally carried on the bike.

# 15. The Politics of Bicycle Commuting

In this final chapter we shall consider the aspects that may improve the lot of the commuting cyclist. In addition to the things that are of some real benefit, I must also discuss some of the ineffective proposals that have been put forward at times, and unfortunately are still being raised from time to time, by those who mean well but don't understand. We'll look at both what I call *micro* and *macro* politics: dealing with small units, such as individual employers, and the big ones, such as states, counties and cities, respectively.

In many areas around the country, bicycle user groups have been formed in recent years, usually with names like "... Bicycle Coalition." Unfortunately, only too many of these groups campaign hard and ignorantly for the wrong provisions — including specifically bike paths and traffic restrictions. For a while, even the national cyclist organization LAW (League of American Wheelmen, masquerading under the name Bicycle USA) appeared to be running fast in the wrong direction, a disaster that could be averted before it was too late.

Fortunately the LAW, and some of the more competent and less hysterical local groups, are quite active in lobbying at both levels for better bicycle facilities and improved access. Of the two, please don't forget that for the bicycle commuter the latter is often the more important aspect.

## Bicycle Access
What the bicyclist needs more than anything else is the unrestricted use of the road — not, as some people seem to think, special bike paths someplace where you or I aren't going. Unfortunately, bike path legislation has become a motherhood issue and the large sums spent on them make it all the harder to provide more sensible facilities for cyclists. I have heard arguments like, "We've just provided a bike path around the lake, so go ride there and not on High Street." It so happens that the bicycle commuter probably works on High Street, so that's where he has to ride, not around the lake.

Particularly sensitive are bridges, since they are usually bottlenecks providing the only access to certain areas. Many times, the roads crossing them are either real or *de facto* freeways, which are in most states off limits to bicyclists. Bicycle groups can lobby for solutions to such problems. In some cases, especially when enough lane or shoulder width is available, it is just a

Excellent bike parking racks at a company parking lot. Since this photo was taken, a roof was installed over the bike rack area.

matter of removing the sign prohibiting bicycles from the access roads. In other cases, particularly with narrow lanes and missing paved shoulders, there is a real or perceived safety problem, and in those cases shuttle services, ferries or additional lightly constructed bicycle bridges can provide the answer.

## Parking Facilities

Bike parking is both a micro and a macro political question. On the level of big politics — in terms of our discussion — some cities have provided both public parking and instituted ordinances to make bicycle parking facilities mandatory in all places of business. The California city of Palo Alto is a shining example of such progressive local government.

With the exception just mentioned, the situation at shops and other places of business, as well as places employment, is usually left to the individual, so it will be micro politics for you. Often it is possible to get permission to bring the bike inside and find a place for it there. In my neighborhood; I know where my bike is welcome and I like to do my shopping there, boycotting those stores where I know my bike is unwanted.

At work, the situation depends very much on the attitude of the employer and on the individual cyclist's clout. When I was considered a radical troublemaker, I was forced to park outside — with disastrous results. Later, when I became accepted, or at least when the causes I had always advocated had become so, it was easy to get permission to install bike parking facilities in a safe place in the building. Talk about it and you may be offered adequate parking facilities.

In addition to simple racks to park the bike, such as the fence introduced in Chapter 14, places like railway stations should be equipped with bicycle storage boxes. These are oversized lockers, or miniature garages, that may either be rented by the month or coin operated. They keep the bike dry and hidden from the eyes of the pilfering types who can deduce only too easily that a bike standing about near a train station is not going to see its owner until the evening.

## Bike Paths

I haven't seen many useful bike paths yet, but the pressure is on everywhere to provide these miniature roads for cyclists, or at least designated bike lanes in the existing road. Though the latter are not quite as dangerous as the former, both types have so many problems that I tire of recounting them all. I'll gladly send you a detailed account of their inherent problems, but for the time being, take my word for it that 99 times out of 100 you will be much better off riding the road than any bike path known to man.

One of the most pervasive and dispicable lies about bike paths is the argument that they encourage bicycle use. They don't, as investigation of their history will prove. From Palo Alto and Davis in California to Stevenage and Milton Keynes in Great Britain to Tilburg and The Hague in Holland, they were either built in response to existing high numbers of cyclists (which did *not* increase further isubsequently) or to provide motorists with a clear shot.

If you ever get a chance to visit the British new town of Stevenage, just north of London, you'll be able to confirm that even the best road and path builders in the world don't succeed in turning a town full of bike paths into a town full of cyclists: In Stevenage, people drive their cars to work and kids walk to school, whereas the bicycle commuter is rare indeed there. Ironically, in older communities without separated facilties only thirty miles away bicycle commuting is much more common.

If bike paths are provided, they should at least be built and maintained to the same standards as regular roads — surface qualities, sight lines, curve radii, clearances, the lot. Even so, to use them safely, you will have to ride slower and more carefully than you would on the road. Most importantly, their use should not be compulsory — unfortunately, many states ordain that it is.

In some states bicycles are allowed to use sidewalks and other pedestrian facilities, except that this dubious privilege can be revoked again by local ordinance. No problem to me, since I consider the use of sidewalks even more insane than it is to ride a bike path. Don't, even if you are allowed to, except in such areas where a pedestrian facility provides an obvious short cut. Even then, ride with utmost care, since pedestrian facilities are not designed for the speeds at which bicycles travel. Besides, the pedestrians using them have a right to expect to use their facility without being endangered by you or any other vehicle operator.

Much more useful than bike paths is the width and the quality of the road. Smooth surfaces, paved shoulders and wide RH lanes (or straight through lanes at complex intersections) are useful to cyclists.

### Traffic Control
Many communities have instituted schemes to restrict or guide traffic. Often these plans are intended to force traffic to flow through certain roads to relieve the load on others. This sometimes results in unreasonable detours that may be acceptable to motorists, since they are indeed the cause of the problem and can easily do a mile more here or there. For bicyclists they often seem highly offensive and inap-

propriate. After all, at cycling speeds, a mile here or there is not made up so quickly, and in comparison to the typical trip distance the detour is often disproportionately long. Finally, cycling is not the cause of the problem but the solution.

Even so, in most cases you will find that as long as you can not apply enough pressure to rescind or modify the whole scheme, you'll be better off adhering to it than trying to find other cycling routes — be they officially sanctioned or spontaneous. I have recorded the results of the effects of following the prescribed route as compared to the use of alternatives (including walking across and riding against traffic). In most cases, the time needed for the alternative route was actually more than it would have taken to follow the prescribed route. But what is more alarming, the number of conflict situations to which the alternative route exposed the cyclist invariably far exceeded the number when following the prescribed route.

This should not discourage you from joining with other cyclists and making sure you get heard whenever such a scheme is proposed or when it is up for consideration. But first do your homework. Find an alternative route that would solve the same problem without hindering cyclists as much. Your bicyclist's perspective often helps you observe possibilities that escape those who are used to seeing the world through the windshield of their car.

### Other Issues
The day-to-day work of bicycle commuting involves other traffic related problems as well, where your bicyclist's perspective helps perceive problems that are not otherwise easily noticed. One of them is the state of the road surface. Certainly if you have joined a bicycle group, it will be useful — both to

you and your local road department — to report systematically on specific road damage needing repair. In many cases, the road agency's liability for accidents caused by inadequate road maintenance gives you enough clout to achieve quite a bit.

A good example of this is the problem of drain or sewer grates. These things are needed to drain rain water off the road and are therefore always located close to the curb, where the level is lowest. But that's where many bicyclists spend a good part of their time (though I encourage you to avoid this part of the road whenever the situation allows, you will finish up riding there very often). And the bicycle also happens to be the only vehicle on the road with wheels narrow enough to be endangered if they are installed the wrong way.

The right way to install them is with the slots either perpendicular or diagonal to the road. In many cases they are designed to fit only the wrong way round, i.e. with the slots parallel. And a very tricky thing it is, to get your front wheel stuck in one of these: your front wheel will stop dead and you will go over the handlebars, resulting in all sorts of unpleasant consequences to you and your bike, not to mention the liability to the authority responsible.

Make a list of the exact locations (street, block, side of street, nearest house number or other reference point) and the date first noticed. Present regular updates of this list to the responsible agency with an official cover letter explaining that you notify them of those locations and will expect them to be corrected within 30 days or so. From time to time, check whether the job has been done, so you can cross the corrected ones off your list, while adding the ones you have found since the last update.

You may be told nothing can be done, which is a patent lie. One solution for ex-

isting sewer grates that can only be installed with the slots parallel to the road is to braze flat steel strips over the top going the opposite direction (welding doesn't work on the cast iron typically used for these grates). Whatever the solution is, that's up to the agency responsible, but it helps if *you* at least know what can be done, in case they try to tell you there's no solution.

Though at first things like this may not be welcomed with open arms, you will soon find out that the folks in such offices are human beings too, which they will find out about you as well. Working together with local authorities on this and similar problems has brought many a bicycle group the recognition it deserved. It improves the image of the bicycle commuter, and that's worth it.

Palo Alto bike politician and Vice Mayor Ellen Fletcher with one of her many achievements: bike-up bank teller.

# Appendix

## Table 1 — Frame sizing table

| leg length | | racing | max. seat tube height (A) bike | mountain bike | |
|---|---|---|---|---|---|
| cm | in | cm | in | cm | in |
| 72 | 29 | 50 | 19 | 46 | 17.5 |
| 73 | | 51 | 19.5 | 47 | 18 |
| 74 | | 52 | 20 | 48 | 18.5 |
| 75 | | 52 | 20 | 48 | 18.5 |
| 76 | 30 | 53 | 20.5 | 49 | 19 |
| 77 | | 54 | 21 | 50 | 19.5 |
| 78 | | 55 | 21 | 51 | 19.5 |
| 79 | 31 | 56 | 21.5 | 52 | 20 |
| 80 | | 57 | 22 | 53 | 20.5 |
| 81 | 32 | 58 | 22.5 | 54 | 21 |
| 82 | | 59 | 23 | 55 | 21.5 |
| 83 | | 60 | 23 | 56 | 21.5 |
| 84 | 33 | 61 | 23.5 | 57 | 22 |
| 85 | | 62 | 24 | 58 | 22.5 |
| 86 | 34 | 63 | 24.5 | 59 | 23 |
| 87 | | 64 | 25 | 60 | 23.5 |
| 88 | | 65 | 25 | 61 | 23.5 |
| 89 | 35 | 66 | 25.5 | 62 | 24 |
| 90 | | 67 | 26 | 63 | 24 |
| 91 | 36 | 68 | 26.5 | 64 | 24 |
| 92 | | 69 | 27 | 65 | 24 |

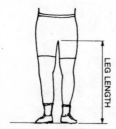
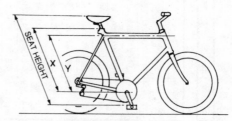

Fig. A. Inseam leg length determination    Fig. B. Frame size determination

*Remarks:*
1. This table applies to bicycles with 26 in, 27 in, 650 mm and 700 mm wheels.
2. Inside leg measurement is taken per Fig. A.
3. Maximum recommended seat height as defined in Fig. B, dimension X. If measured per dimension Y, a nominal frame size must be selected that is 1.5 cm or 0.5 inch smaller.

## Table 2 — Gearing table

number of teeth sprocket

number of teeth chainwheel

| | 12 | 13 | 14 | 15 | 16 | 17 | 18 | 19 | 20 | 21 | 22 | 23 | 24 | 25 | 26 | 28 | 30 |
|---|---|---|---|---|---|---|---|---|---|---|---|---|---|---|---|---|---|
| 56 | 126 | 116.3 | 108 | 100.8 | 94.5 | 88.9 | 84 | 79.5 | 75.6 | 72 | 68.7 | 65.7 | 63 | 60.4 | 58.1 | 54 | 50.2 |
| 55 | 123.7 | 114.2 | 106 | 99 | 92.8 | 87.3 | 82.5 | 78.1 | 74.5 | 70.7 | 67.5 | 64.5 | 61.8 | 59.4 | 57.1 | 53 | 49.4 |
| 54 | 121.5 | 112.1 | 104.1 | 97.2 | 91.1 | 85.7 | 81 | 76.7 | 72.9 | 69.4 | 66.2 | 63.6 | 60.7 | 58.3 | 56 | 52 | 48.6 |
| 53 | 119.3 | 110 | 102.2 | 95.4 | 89.4 | 84.1 | 79.5 | 75.3 | 71.5 | 68.1 | 65 | 62.2 | 59.6 | 57.2 | 55 | 51.1 | 47.5 |
| 52 | 117 | 108 | 100.3 | 93.6 | 87.8 | 82.6 | 78 | 73.9 | 70.2 | 66.9 | 63.8 | 61 | 58.5 | 56.2 | 54 | 50 | 46.8 |
| 50 | 112.3 | 103.9 | 96.4 | 90 | 84.4 | 79.4 | 75 | 71.1 | 67.5 | 64.3 | 61.4 | 58.7 | 56.3 | 54 | 51.9 | 48.2 | 45 |
| 49 | 110.2 | 101.8 | 94.5 | 88.2 | 82.7 | 77.8 | 73.5 | 69.4 | 66.2 | 63 | 60.1 | 57.5 | 55.1 | 52.9 | 50.9 | 47.2 | 44 |
| 48 | 108 | 99.7 | 92.6 | 86.4 | 81 | 76.2 | 72 | 68 | 64.8 | 61.7 | 58.9 | 56.3 | 54 | 51.8 | 49.9 | 46.3 | 43.2 |
| 47 | 105.7 | 97.6 | 90.6 | 84.6 | 79.3 | 74.6 | 70.5 | 66.6 | 63.4 | 60.4 | 57.6 | 55.2 | 52.9 | 50.8 | 48.8 | 45.3 | 42.1 |
| 46 | 103.5 | 95.5 | 88.7 | 82.8 | 77.6 | 73.1 | 69 | 65.3 | 62.1 | 59.1 | 56.5 | 54 | 51.8 | 49.7 | 47.8 | 44.4 | 41.4 |
| 45 | 101.2 | 93.4 | 86.7 | 80.9 | 76 | 71.5 | 67.5 | 64 | 60.8 | 57.9 | 55.2 | 52.8 | 50.7 | 48.6 | 46.7 | 43.7 | 40.5 |
| 44 | 99 | 91.4 | 84.9 | 79.2 | 74.3 | 69.9 | 66 | 62.5 | 59.4 | 56.6 | 54 | 51.6 | 49.5 | 47.5 | 45.7 | 42.4 | 39.6 |
| 42 | 94.5 | 87.2 | 81 | 75.6 | 70.9 | 66.7 | 63 | 59.7 | 56.7 | 54 | 51.5 | 49.3 | 47.3 | 45.4 | 43.6 | 40.5 | 37.5 |
| 40 | 90 | 83.1 | 77.1 | 72 | 67.5 | 63.5 | 60 | 56.8 | 54 | 51.4 | 49.1 | 47 | 45 | 43.2 | 41.5 | 38.6 | 36 |
| 38 | 85.5 | 78.9 | 73.3 | 68.4 | 64.1 | 60.3 | 57 | 54 | 51.3 | 48.9 | 46.6 | 44.6 | 42.8 | 41 | 39.5 | 36.6 | 34.2 |
| 36 | 81.1 | 74.7 | 69.5 | 64.8 | 60.9 | 57.2 | 54 | 51.1 | 48.7 | 46.4 | 44.2 | 42.4 | 40.5 | 38.9 | 37.4 | 34.8 | 32.4 |
| 34 | 76.5 | 70.6 | 65.5 | 61.1 | 57.2 | 54 | 51 | 48.2 | 45.9 | 43.7 | 41.6 | 39.9 | 38.2 | 36.7 | 35.3 | 32.8 | 30.6 |
| 32 | 72 | 66.4 | 61.7 | 57.6 | 54 | 50.8 | 48 | 45.5 | 43.2 | 41.1 | 39.2 | 37.5 | 36 | 34.6 | 33.2 | 30.8 | 28.6 |
| 30 | 67.5 | 62.3 | 57.8 | 54 | 50.6 | 47.6 | 45 | 42.6 | 40.5 | 38.6 | 36.8 | 35.2 | 33.7 | 32.4 | 31.2 | 28.9 | 27 |
| 28 | 63 | 58.1 | 54 | 50.4 | 47.2 | 44.4 | 42 | 39.7 | 37.8 | 36 | 34.3 | 32.8 | 31.5 | 30.2 | 29 | 27 | 25.1 |
| 26 | 58.5 | 54 | 50.1 | 46.8 | 43.7 | 41.2 | 39 | 36.8 | 35.1 | 33.4 | 31.9 | 30.5 | 29.2 | 28 | 27 | 25 | 23.2 |
| 24 | 54.1 | 49.8 | 46.2 | 43.2 | 40.5 | 38.1 | 36 | 34.1 | 32.4 | 30.8 | 29.4 | 28.1 | 27 | 25.9 | 24.9 | 23.1 | 21.6 |

## Table 3 — Development conversion graph

Gear number (inches)

```
  30   40   50   60   70   80   90   100  110  120   in
  |||||||||||||||||||||||||||||||||||||||||||||||||||||
 2,0   3,0   4,0   5,0   6,0   7,0   8,0   10,0  11,0   m
```

Development (meters)

# Bibliography

Allen, John S. *The Complete Book of Bicycle Commuting.* Emmaus, PA: Rodale Press, 1981.

Cross, Kenneth and Gary Fisher. *A Study of Bicycle/Motor Vehicle Accidents.* Washington DC: National Highway Traffic Safety Administration, 1977.

Forester, John. *Bicycle Transportation.* Cambridge, MS: MIT-Press, 1986.

———. *Effective Cycling.* Cambridge, MS: MIT-Press, 1985.

Franklin, John. *Cyclecraft: Skilled cycling techniques for adults.* London (GB): Unwin, 1988.

Institute of Transportation Engineers. *Transportation and Traffic Engineering Handbook.* Englewood Cliffs, NJ: Prentice-Hall, 1976.

Kaplan, Jerrold A. *Characteristics of the Regular Adult Bicycle Usser.* Springfield, VA: National Technical Information Service, 1976.

*Motorcycle Roadcraft, The police rider's manual.* London (GB): HMSO, 1978 (Though written for motorcyclist training, the approach of this book makes it almost equally useful to bicyclists.)

Van der Plas, Rob. *The Penguin Bicycle Handbook.* Harmondsworth (GB): Penguin Books, 1983.

Wolfe, Frederick L.. *The Bicycle A Commuting Alternative.* Edmonds. WA: Signpost Books, 1979.

# Index

# Other Books from Bicycle Books, Inc.

**MAJOR TAYLOR**
**The extraordinary career of a champion bicycle racer**
**Andrew Ritchie**

304 pages (6x9) plus 32-page photo insert
ISBN 0-933201-14-1, hardcover

The fascinating story of Major Taylor, the black American professional bicycle racer who was the world's most popular sportsman around the turn of the century.

**THE BICYCLE RACING GUIDE**
**Technique and training for bicycle racers and triathletes**
**Rob van der Plas**

256 pages (6x9) with over 250 illustrations
ISBN 0-933201-13-3, paperback

This is the most complete and authoritative guide to training for bicycle racing for beginner and advanced rider alike. This book was selected for the US travelling sports book expo during the 1988 Olympics and received international acclaim.

**IN HIGH GEAR**
**The world of professional bicycle racing**
**by Samuel Abt**

192 pages (6x9) text plus 16-page photo insert
ISBN 0-933201-24-5 Hardcover
ISBN 0-933201-25-7 Paperback

The inside story on the international bicycle racing scene and the life of the professional bike racer.

**THE BICYCLE FITNESS BOOK**
**Using the bike for health and fitness**
**Rob van der Plas**

144 pages (6x9) with over 80 illustrations
ISBN 0-933201-23-0, paperback

Cycle for fitness. This book shows exactly how to select the right bike, clothes and other equipment, how to ride and how to train.

**THE MOUNTAIN BIKE BOOK**
**Choosing, riding and maintaining the off-road bicycle**
**Rob Van der Plas**

208 pages (6x9) with 250 illustrations
ISBN 0-933201-18-4, paperback

The second edition of Bicycle Books' first title. Acknowledged to be the best book of its kind. Fully updated and expanded.

## THE BICYCLE REPAIR BOOK
### The complete manual of bicycle care
### Rob Van der Plas

140 pages (6x9) with 300 illustrations
ISBN 0-933201-11-7, paperback

Easily the best general bicycle repair manual on the market today. This book is kept fully updated each time it is reprinted.

### The Bicycle Touring Manual
### Using the bicycle for touring and camping
### Rob Van der Plas

272 pages (6x9) with over 250 illustrations
ISBN 0-933201-15-X, paperback

This book covers all aspects of touristic cycling, from selecting bike and other equipment to planning your route and finding the way both at home and abroad.

## MOUNTAIN BIKE MAINTENANCE
### Repairing and maintaining the off-road bicycle
### Rob Van der Plas

112 pages (6x9) with over 120 illustrations
ISBN 0-933201-22-2

This new manual provides well illustrated step-by-step instructions for all the maintenance work on the ATB, or mountain bike.

## ROADSIDE BICYCLE REPAIRS
### The simple guide to fixing your bike
### Rob Van der Plas

112 pages (6 x 4 $^1/2$) with over 100 illustrations
ISBN 0-933201-16-8, paperback

This handy pocket-size book provides all the information needed to carry out necessary repairs while riding the bike. Ideal for the non-technically inclined.

## THE NEW BIKER'S BOOK
### Understanding and using your bike
### Jim Langley

### NEW: March 1990
128 pages (6 x 4 $^1/2$) with 50 illustrations
ISBN 0-933201-30-8, paperback

Here's the book for every man or woman new to cycling. Explains the essentials without getting bogged down in technical details that don't interest most new cyclists.

**Bicycle Technology**
**The complete technical manual for the modern bicycle**
**Rob Van der Plas**

**NEW: June 1990**
224 pages (6x9) with over 300 illustrations
ISBN 0-933201-31-6, hardcover

This impressive book wraps up all there is to know about the technical aspects of the modern bicycle. A reference work of lasting value.

# How to Order Books from Bicycle Books, Inc.

All books published by Bicycle Books, Inc. may be obtained through the book or bike trade. If not available locally, order directly from the publisher. Allow three weeks for shipping. Mail coupon to:

**Bicycle Books, Inc.**
P. O. Box 2038
Mill Valley, CA 94941
Tel.: (415) 381 0172
FAX: (415) 381 6912

Please enclose payment in full (check or money order made payable to Bicycle Books, Inc.) Books not paid for in advance will be sent UPS COD.

**Canadian and other foreign customers please note:**
All prices quoted are US $ prices and must be paid in advance with check drawn on US bank or International Money Order – no COD available on foreign orders. Shipping charge $2.50 (or $4.50 Air Mail) per book.

**Please send the following book(s):** ☐ Check here if payment is enclosed

|  | | | |
|---|---|---|---|
| The Mountain Bike Book | ___ copies @ $9.95 = | $ ___ |
| The Bicycle Repair Book | ___ copies @ $8.95 = | $ ___ |
| The Bicycle Racing Guide | ___ copies @ $10.95 = | $ ___ |
| The Bicycle Touring Manual | ___ copies @ $10.95 = | $ ___ |
| Roadside Bicycle Repairs | ___ copies @ $4.95 = | $ ___ |
| Major Taylor (hardcover) | ___ copies @ $19.95 = | $ ___ |
| Bicycling Fuel | ___ copies @ $7.95 = | $ ___ |
| In High Gear (hardcover) | ___ copies @ $16.95 = | $ ___ |
| In High Gear (paperback) | ___ copies @ $10.95 = | $ ___ |
| Mountain Bike Maintenance | ___ copies @ $7.95 = | $ ___ |
| The Bicycle Fitness Book | ___ copies @ $7.95 = | $ ___ |
| The Bicycle Commuting Book | ___ copies @ $7.95 = | $ ___ |
| The New Biker's Book | ___ copies @ $4.95 = | $ ___ |
| Bicycle Technoglogy (hardcover) | ___ copies @ $19.95 = | $ ___ |

**Sub total** $ ___
California residents add 6% (6.5%) sales tax $ ___
Postage and handling $2.00 first book,
$1.00 each additional book (within US) $ ___

**Total amount** $ ___

Name:_____
Address:_____
City, state, zip: _____  Tel.: ( ___ ) _____